Bogong National Park, Victoria

National Parks of Victoria, South Australia & Tasmania

National Parks of Victoria, South Australia & Tasmania

READER'S DIGEST

The editors wish to thank the officers of the Department
of Conservation Forests and Lands of Victoria, and the National Parks and
Wildlife Services of South Australia and Tasmania for their advice and assistance; in particular, Sandra Bardwell,
Ann Prescott, Leonie Heard and Rodney Musch.

Some of the material in this book first appeared in
Reader's Digest Wild Australia, first published in 1984.

**WILD AUSTRALIA was edited and designed by
Reader's Digest Services Pty Limited**

All travelling photographic commissions were
undertaken by Robin Morrison

Project Editor   Art Editor
David Underhill   Anita Sattler

Editor • Robert Campbell
Assistant Editor • Francoise Toman
Research Editor • Vere Dodds

READER'S DIGEST NATIONAL PARKS OF VICTORIA, SOUTH AUSTRALIA AND TASMANIA
was edited and designed by Reader's Digest Services Pty Ltd

Project Editor   **Art Editor**
Shirley Macnab   Anita Sattler

FIRST EDITION
Published by Reader's Digest Services Pty Limited (Inc. in NSW)
26-32 Waterloo Street, Surry Hills, NSW 2010
Some of the material in this book first appeared in
Reader's Digest Wild Australia, first published in 1984.
© 1987 Reader's Digest Services Pty Limited
© 1987 Reader's Digest Association Far East Limited
Philippines copyright 1987 Reader's Digest Association Far East Limited
All rights reserved. No part of this book may be reproduced, stored in
a retrieval system, or transmitted by any form or by any means,
electronic, magnetic tape, mechanical, photocopying, recording or
otherwise without permission in writing from the publishers.

National Library of Australia cataloguing-in-publication data
National parks of Victoria, South Australia and Tasmania.

Includes index.
ISBN 0 86438 039 9.

1. National parks and reserves – Victoria –
Guide-books. 2. National parks and reserves – South
Australia – Guide-books. 3. National parks and reserves
– Tasmania – Guide-books. 4. Victoria – Description and
travel – 1976- – Guide-books. 5. South Australia –
Description and travel – 1976- – Guide-books.
6. Tasmania – Description and travel – 1976- –
Guide-books. I. Reader's Digest Services.

919.4'04

CONTENTS

Introduction 7

PART ONE:

The nature of Australia 8

How the stage was set 10

Sun and rain: the great dictators 12

Grandeur in the high country 14

Fresh water: a precious bounty 16

Where the oceans hold sway 18

The eternal battle of the trees 20

Rainforests: a squandered heritage 22

The forests that welcome fire 24

Sentinels of the never-never 26

PART TWO:

Parks and people 28

Why we have national parks 30

Jacks and Jills of all trades 32

Staying alive in the bush 34

How the public can help 36

Making the most of your visit 37

WILDLIFE: Where animals find safety 38

RESTORATION: Nature gets another chance 40

HERITAGE: An obligation to the world 42

PART THREE:

A guide to the national parks of Victoria, South Australia & Tasmania 44

ADELAIDE REGION 46

Directory of parks 67

South Australian wildlife 70

VISITOR ACTIVITIES 74

MELBOURNE REGION 76

Directory of parks 110

Victoria's wildlife 114

VISITOR ACTIVITIES 118

LAUNCESTON & DEVONPORT REGIONS 120

Directory of parks 132

DAM CONFRONTATION: How the west was won 134

HOBART REGION 136

Directory of parks 151

Plants in Tasmania's parks 152

VISITOR ACTIVITIES 156

Index 158

Acknowledgments 160

Port Campbell National Park, Victoria

INTRODUCTION

What's in a name?

AUSTRALIA HAS more than 500 so-called national parks. Their status was proclaimed by state and territorial authorities under policies that used to differ widely. Many parks, especially among the 300-odd declared in Queensland, are mere islets or scraps of bush as small as one hectare. Some are huge, but so remote and inhospitable that their existence has little public relevance. And in a few parks, visitors have no place at all – the sites are really animal sanctuaries, or strictly for scientific research.

Nature reserves of that sort are important. But people expect direct benefits from something called a national park. The term should denote a significant area capable of accommodating the right of substantial numbers of visitors to enjoy its natural features and learn from them. Too many 'parks' do not meet this prescription. Bestowed indiscriminately, a proud title loses meaning. The effect, though surely not intended, is sometimes to mislead and disappoint the public.

In offering a frank comparison of park attractions, we aim not to dictate readers' tastes but to provide them with a fair basis for making choices of their own. This guide, together with its three companion volumes, presents a revision and expansion of information first amassed in the 1984 Reader's Digest book *Wild Australia*. That remains the only single publication to appraise the country's entire array of parks.

Simply identifying all of them demanded a trailblazing effort. Because of the pace of acquisition and change since the 1950s, no complete list had existed. Even the names of some parks were difficult to establish. Legally gazetted titles conflicted with common usage, or hard-pressed administrators saved paperwork by lumping smaller sites anonymously into groups.

Financial strictures beset all parks services. Areas may be designated by the stroke of a pen, but funds for public facilities are a long time coming. Often as our researchers sought to define the merits of a park, they were told: 'We'd really rather you didn't mention that one'. A state information officer, confessing his ignorance of a newly acquired property, explained: 'We sent a fellow out there once to get material for a brochure. But he couldn't find the place...'

Not without qualms, a system of rating was instituted. Judgments behind all the ticks and crosses in the reference sections were made in consultation with park authorities, but they remain subjective and debatable. So are our assumptions of the broad areas of visitor interest. 'Scenic enjoyment' in one park derives from the intimate charm of a single waterfall; in another it may come from the sweeping grandeur of a whole mountain range or coastline. 'Day activities' indicates a good choice of things to do – but who can predict preferences? 'Family camping' supposes a desire to stay put for perhaps a week, in conditions not unduly primitive. 'Hard bushwalking' in most cases points to the challenge of backpack trekking and overnight camping.

Pictorially we have aimed for realism, not idealism. Rather than gathering in a selection of the prettiest and luckiest shots ever taken in national parks, we offer the results of one man's efforts. Robin Morrison, the touring photographer, was advised and guided by rangers in some parks. But for the most part he took his chances like any other member of the travelling public, limited in time and at the mercy of the weather.

After his year-long assignment for *Wild Australia*, covering more than 200 locations from Tasmania to North West Cape, Morrison had a suggestion. 'Tell your readers,' he said, 'that anything I did, they can do. With any luck they may see even more. And you can also tell them that most of the finest scenery in this country is not all that far away or hard to get to.'

He was right. In spite of the obvious modification of desirable countryside by two centuries of European settlement, unspoilt landscapes lie remarkably close to most major centres of population. Australians, nearly 90 per cent of whom lead their everyday lives in urban or suburban environments, need not go far to refresh themselves and recover their sense of community with more natural surroundings.

This guide and the others in the series are published in the hope that readers will reach a fuller understanding of what remains of our physical heritage, that they will care for it, and above all that they will enjoy it.

THE EDITORS

PART ONE
The nature of Australia

Nothing in nature happens without a reason. Powerful influences shaped Australia's landscapes. Now they dictate where its unique plants grow. Knowing the meaning that lies behind scenery makes it all the more enjoyable.

Ancient but scarcely trodden, the Bungle Bungle Ranges stand in lonely dignity east of the Kimberleys, WA

THE NATURE OF AUSTRALIA
How the stage was set

WEATHERING, given time enough, levels any land surface. Heights are worn down and basins are filled with the debris, to be compressed into fresh rock. With the ups and downs removed and gravity equalised, rock erosion stops. Only overlying soils or sands are subject to further attack.

But awesome pressures work tirelessly on the earth's crust. Sometimes they warp it, tilting an old land mass to a new angle of elevation. Sometimes the crust buckles, and another generation of mountains is thrust up. Molten material from below blasts or oozes through weak points in the crust. The height of the land is varied and erosion resumes. All these events have occurred time and again in Australia.

Rocks of the Australian land mass differ astonishingly in their age, their composition and their capacity to resist erosion. They include the world's oldest known formations as well as some of the youngest, and everything from the softest clays to the most impermeable granites. Climatic conditions vary widely. So do the surrounding oceans in their behaviour – some destroy the land, some help it to build. Most diverse of all are the soils produced by rock erosion, and the plant life they can sustain.

Flat landscapes, virtually featureless and usually parched, prevail across more than half of the continent. Weathering is all but complete, for much of this land has been undisturbed for eons. Ranges thrust up in the west, made from rocks that formed more than 3000 million years ago, are reduced to a smoothed shield, rarely outcropping from its sandy cover. Once-mighty rivers that drained the heights – and helped demolish them – can be traced only in chains of dismal salt pans. Seabeds to the east have become plains, at best marginally fertile.

Remnants of mountain systems in Central Australia and the far north and northwest are younger, though the age of their rocks still staggers the mind. Ranges such as the Musgraves and the Hamersleys, along with many in the Kimberleys and Arnhem Land, originated more than 1000 million years ago. Pushed up, they towered higher than Mt Kosciusko is now. All are in the late stages of destruction – but nature has not wasted them.

By the time the MacDonnell Ranges were forced up in Central Australia, perhaps 200-300 million years ago, material eroded from the Musgraves had re-formed as a bed of sedimentary rock. South of the MacDonnells, it was distorted and broken by their upheaval. Immense chunks of sandstone or cemented boulders were elevated at all angles, to be swamped later by a returning sea. New deposits of sediments buried all but the highest summits. Now, severely worn in their turn, the broad domes we call Ayers Rock and the Olgas jut incongruously from the central plain.

Nearby Mt Conner, similarly created, presents a surprising contrast. It is table-topped, and noticeably eroded only at the sides. When this mass was pushed up, its layers of sediments chanced to remain horizontal under their original capping of toughened material. To the north, on apparently similar country, are piled the huge boulders called the Devil's Marbles. Here a cracked block of granite has been eroded across and down all its joints. Such variations are essentially the products of chance – what types of rocks are exposed, and how their former bedding planes are tilted.

Ocean levels rose and fell – or the land fell and rose – repeatedly. Invading seas often divided ancestral Australia into islands. New rock material included increasing quantities of calcium from the remains of marine animals. Pavings of porous limestone formed widely. High and dry now, many are noted for their subterranean cave systems, eaten out by percolating rainwater.

Sometimes the seas were remarkably warm. Corals built reefs in the Gordon River district of Tasmania 350-400 million years ago. But 100 million years later an icecap reached to the Kimberleys, and Tasmania lay beside the South Pole. And after a further 100 million years, according to plant fossil evidence, Australia and Antarctica shared a subtropical climate. Like all continental land masses, they have been on the move.

At first all the continents were probably contained in a single cluster, which seems to have broken in two well over 200 million years ago. After that Australia, Antarctica, New Guinea, India, Africa, Arabia and South America were joined in a southern supercontinent which scientists call Gondwanaland. But the earth's rigid crust was fracturing. Rifts opened, and new molten matter welled up to force the modern continents apart.

Widening oceans filled the gaps. The crust

Eroded rock layers at Kings Canyon, NT, are tilted almost vertically. Once they formed towering domes

TRACING A VANISHED LANDSCAPE

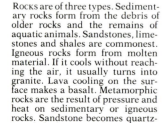

ROCKS are of three types. Sedimentary rocks form from the debris of older rocks and the remains of aquatic animals. Sandstones, limestones and shales are commonest. Igneous rocks form from molten material. If it cools without reaching the air, it usually turns into granite. Lava cooling on the surface makes a basalt. Metamorphic rocks are the result of pressure and heat on sedimentary or igneous rocks. Sandstone becomes quartzite, shale becomes slate, granite becomes gneiss.

Sedimentary rocks form in flat layers, varying in hardness. Squeezed by earth movements, they bend into folds. Erosion removes the softer material in a fold, and only the stubs of tough ridges remain

Molten material pushing up into a fold forms granite. Erosion leaves a tough core (left). But if the material builds a volcano, the last of it may set as a hard-wearing plug of trachyte or rhyolite (right)

Beds of metamorphic rock are too rigid to fold. Instead they crack into blocks that are tilted and pushed up. Rates of erosion depend on the angle of tilt, as well as on the composition of the blocks

The west's ancient granite shield snapped near Perth

itself separated into mobile plates. Fifteen major plates and a few small ones now restlessly cover the globe. The section Australia rides on – along with India, New Guinea and part of New Zealand – is rafting very slowly northwestward because its eastern and southern neighbours are expanding.

Violent earth movements are inevitable at the edges of a plate. But Australia lies far from any collision zone. Since its isolation it has been the least disturbed of the continents. The last truly catastrophic event – the production of eastern and central Tasmania's dolerite columns and cappings by the intrusion of molten matter into old sandstones – was about 165 million years ago. Many geologists associate it with the start of the Gondwanaland breakup.

Early mountain ranges on the eastern mainland were well worn down by then. Soon all that remained of them were cores of tough granite, solidified from molten material that had flowed up into their folds. Often it is this granite that forms the summits of mountains that have been thrust up more recently.

Parts of the Eastern Highlands – notably the Snowy Mountains and Victorian Alps – were pushed up about 65 million years ago. A second phase of general uplift in the east, remarkably gentle, took place within the past 3-7 million years. A probable cause was the slumping of the crust far inland, under the weight of sediments from one ocean or sea after another. The slumped parts, since covered by more recent porous rock, underlie the reservoirs of underground water known collectively as the Great Artesian Basin.

To compensate for this sinking of the crust, land near the east coast gradually rose. It formed tablelands with a barely perceptible slope. Warping to create mountain ranges occurred only in the last stages of uplift, and at the seaward extremity. Similar forces working in the west had a more drastic effect. There the ancient rock shield was pinned down by coastal sediments. It snapped at the point where it emerged, and now its uptilted edge forms a rampart nearly 1000 km long backing the coastal plain on which Perth is centred. The Darling Range is misnamed – it should be the Darling Scarp. But in its influence on climate and vegetation, it acts in much the same way as a mountain system would.

Near-coastal ranges and the coastlines themselves have the freshest and most changeable landforms. All the forces of erosion are seen actively at work. Volcanic activity can be traced. So can the variation of soil fertilities, and the rivalries of plant communities under different climatic regimes. Everywhere, the lie of the land and the look of the landscape are intimately related.

Electric probing mars a history-making zircon – enlarged 200 times

THE OLDEST THING ON EARTH

OUR PLANET was born 4500-4600 million years ago, astronomers believe. It took an unknown time to cool enough to form a solid crust. The most ancient rocks found, in Western Australia and Greenland, are about 3800 million years old. But they are sedimentary – made of something even older.

A clue emerged in 1983 at Mt Narryer, 200 km inland from Carnarvon, WA. Microscopic grains of zircon were discovered in quartzite rocks.

Using a new electrical probing technique, scientists measured the proportions of uranium and lead contained as impurities in the zircons.

Uranium loses its radioactivity and turns into lead at a known rate. So the age of the zircons could be calculated. Four of the tiny stones, it seems, must have been formed between 4100 and 4200 million years ago. Until humans venture outside this solar system, they may never handle anything older.

THE NATURE OF AUSTRALIA

Sun and rain: the great dictators

JUST AS ancient weathering shaped the land, present climates decide its clothing. Sunlight, temperature and moisture determine which trees or shrubs or grasses flourish where. And they govern the likelihood of wildfire – the other factor that sets apart the great plant families of Australia and rules over the appearance of natural landscapes.

Twisting statistics, Australians could boast the world's most generous share of rain. More of it falls, per person, than in any other country. But that is merely a reflection of the sparseness of population. In fact most of the continent is poorly watered and subject to high rates of evaporation. Over a vast sweep between southwestern Queensland and North West Cape, hot sunshine beats down for more than 3500 hours a year.

Mainland Australia straddles the southern hemisphere's belt of greatest air pressure. 'Highs' – cells of descending air as much as 4000 km wide, calm or rotating gently under clear skies – pass from west to east in an almost continuous chain. Troughs separating them, usually at intervals of four or five days, may bring cool changes but seldom much rain. North of the pressurised belt southeasterly breezes – the Trade Winds of sailing ship days – blow steadily from the Pacific. To the south of the belt the air flow is from the west, and much stronger.

The high-pressure belt changes its position seasonally. In winter it is centred over the middle of the continent. Tropical regions, except on the east coast, are parched. The southeasterlies, having deposited their ocean moisture on the coastal ranges, flow on unimpeded and arrive in the northwest dry, hot and dusty.

Southern Australia in winter is swept by a cold westerly air stream. Often this is whipped into chilling southwesterly gales because 'lows' – tight, churning cells of rising and condensing air – intrude from the Southern Ocean. Rain is plentiful, except round the Bight, and the southeastern highlands get snow. But in much of New South Wales and subtropical Queensland, where the westerlies have dried out or do not reach, winter may be sunny.

In summer the belt of high pressure lies over Bass Strait. Rainfall is generally low in southern regions, though clear spells may be broken by squally changes. On most parts of the east coast down to Sydney, however, Pacific moisture is turned into liberal summer rains because the Trade Winds have also moved south.

From November to April, the far north has its 'Wet'. A zone of low pressure, originating over the Equator but shifting in summer to about the latitude of Darwin, sucks in a monsoon of saturated air from the northwest. Thundery showers drench the Kimberleys, the Top End and Cape York Peninsula day after day. In some seasons, but never predictably, the lows pass far enough south to bring flooding rains to Central Australia and outback regions of the southern and eastern states.

Summer is also the season of violent tropical cyclones. Only five or six a year affect the coast, and their destructive power wanes as soon as they pass inland. But the spiralling cloud mass of a decaying cyclone brings heavy rain over an ever-widening area, perhaps for a week or more. Semi-arid regions, particularly in the northwest, receive much of their moisture in this erratic way.

Regardless of average patterns, year-by-year rainfall over most of Australia is notoriously variable. Port Hedland, WA, for example, is listed as having a median annual fall of just over 300 mm. But that figure is merely the product of actual readings as low as 30 mm a year and as high as 1000 mm or more. Apart from the monsoon zone, rainfall is consistently good only in Tasmania, on most of the Victorian, New South Wales and Queensland coasts, and in winter in the extreme southwest of Western Australia. It is no coincidence that all these regions have mountains close to the sea.

Air flowing off sunlit oceans is always loaded with evaporated moisture. But to condense into clouds that precipitate rain, it must be cooled. The usual cause of cooling is elevation: air temperatures drop by about 5°C with each 1000 metres of altitude. A fall in pressure when air flows into a 'low', or a collision of different air masses, can cause the necessary uplift and trigger a storm. However, no one can say exactly where that will happen. Truly reliable rains occur only where moist air flows are blocked and forced upward by steep land.

Australia is not only the flattest of all continents, but also the lowest-lying. Counting mountain ranges, its average elevation is still a mere 300 metres above sea level. That makes it generally warmer than any other land mass in comparable latitudes. Far from being cooled, moist air flowing into many regions is heated up. The longer its journey, the hotter it gets – hence the heat waves that occasionally sear southern cities, including Hobart.

Summer northwesterlies, entering over the Great Sandy Desert between Port Hedland and Broome, have the longest possible low, flat run. If not diverted by atmospheric disturbances they can reach all the way to western NSW – 2500 km. Shade temperatures above 50°C are recorded there, in an arc from Bourke to Wilcannia and White Cliffs, more often than in any other district in Australia.

Superheated air flows hasten the evaporation of soil moisture and the desiccation of plants. In regions perennially short of rain – though with fertile soil – plant life has had to adapt in unusual ways. And where rains in most years are good enough to foster profuse growth, but they occasionally fail, the chance of devastation by fire is abnormally high. Again plants have found ways to cope – and even to benefit.

At the opposite end of the climatic scale, wide tracts of high country in the southeast and Tasmania lie under snow for months each year. Elsewhere, over a surprising area, plants contend with frost in winter and spring. In the south it results from inflows of chilled air after depressions. But frosts also occur well to the north, in places better known for their heat. In the high-pressure belt dominating mid-Australia in winter, cloud cover is rare and ground warmth starts passing into the upper atmosphere as soon as the sun goes down. Alice Springs has more frosty nights than any of the southern capitals except Canberra. On the east coast, the effects of elevation take frosts even farther north. Cooled air, sinking into valleys draining the Great Dividing Range, can ice the ground within 20 km of Cairns.

Parched, sunburnt sandplains reach into NSW at Mungo National Park – once part of a major waterway

Below: Air cooling over Kosciusko National Park, NSW, sinks into the upper Murray Valley, forming a river of cloud

Right: Highland frost and vigorous tree growth join forces to crack capping rock in Girraween National Park, Qld

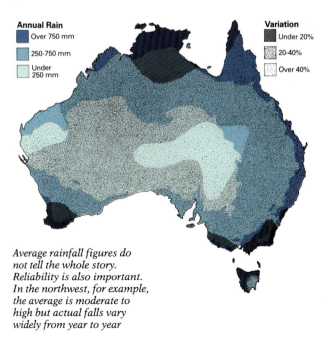

Average rainfall figures do not tell the whole story. Reliability is also important. In the northwest, for example, the average is moderate to high but actual falls vary widely from year to year

THE NATURE OF AUSTRALIA
Grandeur in the high country

MOUNTAINS are nature's showcases. Bared, they display every type and formation of rock. Erosion can be seen in action, with the effects of rain, wind, frost and chemical change accentuated by the force of gravity. And on vegetated slopes, the temperature gradients created by altitude give plant and animal life their fullest opportunity for variety.

Australia lacks the soaring peaks of the other continents and even of its island neighbours, New Guinea and New Zealand. In compensation, its high country is more accessible and less subject to dangerously sudden switches of weather. Its coastal uplands, especially in Queensland, offer a range of plant communities as wide as any in the world.

Scenically and economically, the Eastern Highlands chain is Australia's most significant mountain system. It curves from Cape York into western Victoria, more or less parallel to the coast, and resumes in Tasmania. Islands in Bass and Torres Straits, along with some off Queensland, are peaks emerging from drowned sections of the same system.

For most of their mainland length the highlands are the more elevated seaward side of a wide belt of tablelands. The Great Divide – where rivers start to flow inland, not to the Pacific Ocean – often occurs at lower altitudes well to the west. That shows how slowly the highlands rose in their final uplift, which was completed about 3 million years ago. Ancient rivers, already flowing east, had time to cut deeper courses as the land tipped up.

Movement was so gentle that buckling to produce ranges of fold mountains was limited to the eastern edge of the belt. Massive tilting of fractured blocks, to raise processions of peaks like the Southern Alps of New Zealand, was virtually non-existent. A spectacular exception is the Bellenden Ker Range, just south of Cairns, Qld. Even the summits of the Snowy Mountains and Victorian Alps are smooth granite tablelands. The Blue Mountains, west of Sydney, were just as flat. Layers of sandstone and shale were pushed up thousands of metres without shifting from their horizontal plane. Today's dramatic pillars, cliffs and ravines are simply the result of weathering – and it is far from finished.

Remnants of huge volcanic systems abound, especially about the Qld/NSW border and to the southwest in the Nandewar and Warrumbungle Ranges. These date from 15-25 million years ago. The later phase of eastern uplift brought new activity, but no big volcanoes were built. Most eruptions were easy upwellings of lava from fissures in the earth's crust.

Left: Glaciers sculpted the jagged peaks and walled lakes of southwest Tasmania

Most of the Great Dividing Range is a tableland cut by rivers – in this case the Shoalhaven River in Morton National Park, NSW

Worn quartzite domes in the Gammon Ranges, SA

Hard basalt from ancient lava flows caps Mt Wilson, 950 metres up in Blue Mountains National Park, NSW

Lava flows continued, in fewer and fewer places, almost to the present day. The last coatings on the western plains of Victoria, where more than 20 000 square kilometres are covered, were laid less than 6000 years ago. Even more of the northern Queensland tablelands was blanketed not long before.

Old volcanoes are often marked now by cylinders of rock jutting into the sky. These are plugs made of the last molten material, solidified before it reached the air. It forms exceptionally hard rock – usually trachyte or rhyolite – that resists erosion while the surrounding cone is worn away.

Molten material that flows out as lava, however, turns into a basalt. Its hardness will vary according to its mineral content. Some basalts, reddish or chocolate brown and rich in iron, remain as protective cappings on tablelands or form thin bands sandwiched in the joints of older rocks. Others, cooling evenly in deep layers, have contracted into clusters of tough hexagonal columns – Melbourne's Organ Pipes, for example.

But many basalts decompose quickly when exposed to air and water. They break down into fine, dark soils containing an unusual abundance of mineral nutrients for plants. It is the prevalence of basaltic – often called volcanic – soils, allied with high rainfall, that allows the Eastern Highlands their luxuriant growth of forests.

Tasmania's heights reveal a much older geological background. The region's main upheaval came 165 million years ago. Enormous tongues of molten material penetrated its original sandstone strata. They cooled as dolerite, which has a columnar 'organ pipe' structure similar to some basalts. Now, with almost all of the sandstone worn away, deep sheets of dolerite cover most of eastern and central Tasmania. Sheer-faced crags jut from a tableland so toughly capped that no rivers of significance have managed to cut courses. Instead this is a landscape sculpted by ice. Only in Tasmania can the full effects of glaciation during the last ice age, between 40 000 and 10 000 years ago, be seen. Mountains are chewed away at their sides. Moraines of rock debris trap deep alpine lakes. Countless little tarns, gouged by boulders dragged in a creeping cap of ice, glitter on the plateau.

West of the tableland, Tasmania's ranges have no intrusion of dolerite. They are of softer quartzite, now deeply dissected by gorges. High volumes of water, precipitated almost year-round in rain and snow, seize their chance to find steep courses to the sea between thickly forested slopes. Here are born the island's fast-flowing 'wild rivers', so enticing and precious to white-water adventurers.

No other mountains in Australia stand as tall as the Eastern Highlands, or have soils and rainfall to sustain comparable forest growth. Elsewhere the greatest fascination of higher country usually lies in its stark antiquity. The huge island-mountains of Uluru National Park, for example, or the eroded forms of the Flinders Ranges in South Australia, are individually more haunting than any eastern scene.

Major ranges in Central Australia and the northwest, such as the MacDonnells, the Hamersleys and those in the Kimberleys, are so aged and weathered that their heights lend them little distinction. Instead it is their depths, in the gorges cut by eons-old rivers, which provide the most memorable scenes – and the clearest insights into the structure of the continent.

THIS WAS THE HOTTEST SPOT OF ALL

MOUNT WARNING (left) is the 22-million-year-old central plug of Australia's biggest volcano. Remnants of its rim, straddling the Qld/NSW border across a diameter of about 40 km, survive in the McPherson, Tweed and Nightcap Ranges. All have steep scarps of tough basalt facing in towards Mt Warning, and gently sloping outer flanks.

Scientists can only guess at the original dimensions of the Tweed volcano, but it almost certainly stood taller than Mt Kosciusko is now. Rainforests ringing the rim, largely preserved in a chain of national parks, flourish on rich soils derived from the volcano's outpourings of lava. It is thought to have been active for about 3 million years.

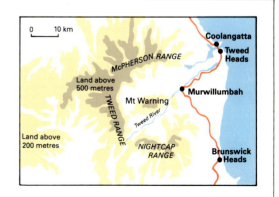

THE NATURE OF AUSTRALIA

Fresh water: a precious bounty

RIVERS AND LAKES are scarce in Australia. Truly natural ones are even more rare. The Aborigines accepted that most water supplies were sporadic: the movements of the animals they hunted, and their own nomadic lives, were ruled by that fact. But European settlers chose accessible rivers and stayed put. They demanded that the water come to them – tamed.

Dams, weirs and levees were built to eliminate the extremes of drought and flood. Banks were straightened and obstacles removed to aid navigation. Flows were diverted to water livestock and irrigate crops. Supplies were drawn off not just for drinking and washing but also for industrial processes, and lately to fill hundreds of thousands of swimming pools.

Even in remote high country, a century or more ago, streams were altered by erosion of their headwater catchments. Forest logging was to blame. More recently, hydro-electric engineering has regulated many rivers, and created new lakes or raised old ones.

Queensland's Barron Falls, once the year-round tourist highlight of the Atherton Tablelands, now flow only in the wet season when the Tinaroo Dam overspills. The Snowy River is deprived of more than 2 million million litres a year by tunnelled diversion to the Murrumbidgee and Murray. The Murray itself is depleted, and salted by the leaching of minerals from cleared land. The Darling, contributing most of the Murray's water, can no longer fluctuate between a chain of billabongs and a flooding sheet hundreds of kilometres wide. Barrages and storage lakes hold it in check.

Where highland rainforests remain untouched, some unspoilt rivers are still to be found flowing in all seasons. Western Tasmania's are the most celebrated – but also the hardest to reach. Many national parks on the Great Dividing Range, however, give access to streams that spill from scarps in waterfalls or cascades, then plunge into ferny ravines.

More indicative of the real nature of most Australian waterways are the braided beds and floodplains of the Channel Country in western Queensland. They are nearly always dry. Even major rivers such as the Diamantina and Cooper Creek are ephemeral, flowing only after prolonged heavy rain. And it takes weeks of the most phenomenal flooding of the Channel Country before the vast salt pans of Lake Eyre are likely to fill.

Monsoon floodplains in the far north are scenes of remarkable annual transformation in plant and animal life. But when it happens, most such districts are inaccessible. The best a traveller can do to appreciate the contrast at Kakadu National Park, for example, is find time for two visits – one just before the wet season, and one as soon as possible after.

Most other national parks in the Northern Terrritory, and all the popular ones to the west from the Kimberleys to Kalbarri, are based on ancient, deeply cut gorges. Their rivers fluctuate seasonally, and in Central Australia most are ephemeral. The attraction for visitors, especially late in the dry season, may be not so much in the watercourses as in the grandeur of their walls. Often the gorges hold pockets of primitive, moist-climate palms and vines – relics of an age long past.

Rivers in the southwest are generally short-flowing and much changed by forest clearance and settlement. Inland, former drainage systems are marked by salt pans, arranged in a horseshoe pattern spanning 500 km. Similar forms extend from north of Lake Eyre to the Flinders Ranges and Eyre Peninsula, SA.

In western NSW, a more recently dried waterway is represented in the Willandra Lakes chain. Mungo National Park's stark lunette walls, like the rims of a moon crater, are built of sands blown from the bed of a lake that held ample water until about 20 000 years ago.

Water storage is so precious now that most natural lakes have been amplified by damming. Australia's deepest, Lake St Clair in Tasmania, was raised to serve power stations on the River Derwent. The greatest of all in area, Lake Argyle in the Kimberleys, was made by damming the Ord River.

Old estuaries, barred by sand ridges, form sizeable coastal lakes in NSW and eastern Victoria. But the streams feeding them are often interfered with, and the lakes themselves modified by settlement or heavy recreational use. Of the few that have been largely spared, outstanding examples are found in The Lakes National Park, Vic, and Myall Lakes National Park, NSW.

The Wimmera River, flowing by Little Desert National Park, gives trees a rare chance in western Victoria

THE HIDDEN RESERVOIRS

ARTESIAN water fell as rain – long ago and very far away. It lies under western Queensland and northwestern NSW, and reaches beneath the Central and South Australian deserts. But all of it came from the Eastern Highlands.

The Great Artesian Basin – really a group of basins separated by underground ridges – is a part of Australia that slumped millions of years ago under the weight of inland seas and their deposits. The sediments formed porous rock, to be capped later by impermeable shales. To balance the slumping, land at the eastern rim rose. Wherever the raised edge of the porous layer has been exposed, it has acted as a conduit for rainwater. Moisture seeps down and collects in a water table, sealed underneath by the old sunken rock.

True artesian water bubbles up under its own pressure if the saturated layer is breached. But bore-sinking for almost a century has lowered the water table; pumping is often needed now. The water is increasingly salty as it ages, and it can have a sulphurous, rotten-egg smell. Most of it is used only for livestock. Where it is pumped from great depths it comes up near-boiling, and can be piped for heating.

Spongy rock exposed near the Great Divide is sandwiched between layers that water cannot penetrate. Rain sinking into it forms a water table extending more than 1500 km southwestward.

Vast floodplains border the Daly River, NT

A VICTORY FOR THE WETLANDS

Hundreds of wildlife species rely on shallow inland waters for at least part of each year. Without swamps and marshes, many would be poorly distributed – and some extinct. But the shrinking wetlands remain targets for reclamation or water diversion.

The trend has been reversed in central NSW, where the Macquarie River spreads into 40 000 ha of meandering creeks and reedy marshes west of Coonamble. The marshes are breeding grounds particularly for ibises, along with more than 150 other species of birds and scores of different amphibians, reptiles and fish.

Upstream, the Burrendong Dam regulates the river. After 1969 the flow was sharply reduced while much of the water went to farms. The river petered out in the marshes, which were impoverished year by year.

Early in the 1980s, a proposed expansion of cotton planting called for even more water to be taken off for irrigation. Protesting conservationists were supported by wheatgrowers and graziers, who had learned that the ibis is a major predator of insects that ruin crops and pastures. The state government heeded their call.

Now the flow to the Macquarie Marshes is almost trebled. Waterfowl habitats are fully flooded, and the river can resume its natural course into the Barwon and on into the Lachlan-Darling-Murray system. The marshes, partly declared as nature reserves and listed by the Heritage Commission, are the likely site of a future national park.

Their waters restored, the Macquarie Marshes come back to life

Left: The last run-off from the summer wet season in the Kimberleys, WA, spills into the Prince Regent River. It flows straight for 80 km along a sandstone fracture

Unspoilt waterways meander through The Lakes National Park, Vic, within easy boating distance of popular Gippsland holiday resorts. The lakes were formed out of estuaries, barred by Ninety Mile Beach

THE NATURE OF AUSTRALIA

Where the oceans hold sway

To see all of Australia's shores at first hand could take a lifetime – or perhaps cost a life. The mainland and Tasmanian coasts, by the most precise measuring method available, extend for more than 30 000 km. Islands on the continental shelf add nearly 18 000 km. Some sections consist of virtually impassable terrain, so far surveyed only from aircraft or boats. Fresh water may not be found for hundreds of kilometres, and the only source of food may be dangerous swamps or seas.

No other country has a coastline so vast, or so pronounced in its contrasts. Shores are backed in some places by deserts, in others by jungles. Towering cliffs and headlands offer seascapes of grandeur; elsewhere the only view may be of mudflats, all the way to the horizon. Ocean currents range from equatorial to subpolar. While seals and Antarctic seabirds breed in the south, warmer waters foster the growth of the world's most massive coral structures.

Australia's coast is noticeably lacking in one respect: for its size, it has very few river outlets. And except near the Eastern Highlands and in the monsoonal north and northwest, rivers have no significant impact on shore formations. There is simply not enough run-off of water or eroded inland rock. Disparity in the supply of material from the hinterland to the coasts, established over millions of years, has led to marked differences in the composition and behaviour of shorelines.

Where plenty of inland material is added to coastal debris, sands are abundant. But they may not stay put. They contain a lot of silica, usually in the form of quartz, so they are slippery. Agitated by waves and winds, they sort themselves until the heaviest minerals – the 'black sands' prized for commercial extraction – lie at the bottom of beaches and dunes. Sands above are light, loose and easily torn away by gales and storm waves.

Coral backs WA's Houtman Abrolhos Islands – once coastal dunes but now 60 km offshore

Right: Lime-rich dunes on the Bight near Penong, SA

On arid shores, sands are composed more of marine sediments. Their higher content of shell and skeleton fragments makes them rich in calcium – a binding agent. Blown inland, these sands pile up and consolidate. Many wave-eroded limestone cliffs, reefs and offshore stacks originated as calcified dune ridges, built when the sea level was lower.

Not all parts of the coast are being eroded. Some hold their own against the sea, or even gain ground. Normal wave power is far from uniform around Australia. It is determined by global weather patterns and the breadth and slope of the continental shelf offshore, as well as by local geography. Waves are generally strongest in the south and ineffectual on tropical shores – except in cyclones. In the far north, river silts discharged into quiet shallows are caught in mangroves to make new land.

Wave direction is important, especially to the fate of beaches. Strong waves breaking at an acute angle to a beach create a powerful longshore current. Washed-off sand is carried away parallel to the shoreline. Where this happens consistently, beaches are depleted and the coastline gradually recedes.

Southeasterly winds and waves attack the eastern bulge of the continent with a regularity that makes beach recession a fact of life. Foredune stabilisation and restraints on property development can stop it happening more quickly than necessary, but the process is inevitable. Sand movement up the mid-east coast has been relentless for more than 8000 years, since the sea rose after the last ice age.

The outcome, where the longshore currents weaken at last, is seen in the chain of sand islands off Brisbane, in the richly coloured cliffs north of Noosa, and finally in the huge mass of Fraser Island. Most of the material that built them originated in the Great Dividing Range, perhaps as far south as the Blue Mountains. Similar forces worked on the western seaboard; in almost a mirror image, its old limestone coast is recessed in the south and built out towards the Tropic of Capricorn.

Where strong waves consistently meet a

Silt collects in a tropical tangle

THE MANGROVE KINGDOM: LIVING WITH THE TIDES

Mangroves are trees and shrubs of many different kinds, all adapted to daily flooding by sea water. They restrict their intake of salt by chemical action, or get rid of it through their leaves. Their seeds are spread by the tides.

Australia has nearly 50 species. Most are notable for the aerial root systems that help to anchor them in soft mud. In some, the roots have openings through which the trees breathe when their soils are saturated. Other species send up breathing pegs for metres around each tree.

On northern coasts, communities of 20 of more species form broad, dense forests up to 30 metres tall. Diversity and vigour decline farther south. Around Sydney three or four species form open stands, seldom exceeding 15 metres. In Victoria, South Australia and south of Perth there is only the grey mangrove, stunted and sparsely distributed.

Boat users and resort developers may see mangroves as nuisances. But they stabilise shorelines by trapping silt in their tangled roots. And their fallen leaves start an estuarine food chain on which marine animals – including most commercially harvested fish – depend. Each square metre of tropical mangrove forest yields about 1 kg of organic matter every year.

shore head-on, they can add to the land. They push sand in to form nearshore barriers, sometimes shutting off bays or estuaries. The lagoons that are created eventually fill with silts and windblown sands. Beaches formed of massive barriers occur frequently on the east coast between the Tropic and Wilsons Promontory, and are also found in eastern South Australia and south of Perth.

Tropical Queensland and the Northern Territory, with weaker wave action, have lower barrier beaches less obvious in their origin. Gulfs and landlocked bays in these regions tend to fill as tidal mudflats, backed by broad mangrove beds and salt marshes and sometimes fringed with coral. Open tidal plains, reaching for many kilometres between high and low waterlines, occur widely on each side of North West Cape between Shark Bay and Port Hedland.

Long, open mainland beaches, free of barriers, develop where the general direction of waves is past a shoreline rather than at it. Reefs and rocky sections may give protection, but the sandy stretches predominate. They are common in western Victoria and northern and eastern Tasmania, towards the head of the Bight and in some parts of the southwest.

Headlands interrupt most beach coasts in the southeast, giving shelter and good vantage points. Their bases usually have wave-cut shore platforms, teeming with marine life. Continuously cliffed coasts, however, are rare. The principal ones in accessible areas are immediately south of Sydney – through Royal National Park and beyond – in Otway and Port Campbell National Parks in Victoria, and around most of southeastern Tasmania.

Sheer limestone cliffs give a sharp edge to much of the Nullarbor Plain, and to the desolate western extremity of the continent, north of Kalbarri National Park. The longest rock coast of all skirts the Kimberleys, where red sandstone precipices are cut by fiordlike inlets. Prodigious tides that can range up to 12 metres create channelled currents of freakish violence. And tidal bores – waves that race up rivers – can overturn boats 50 km inland.

Often it is the reefs and islands offshore that most distinguish a coast. They enrich its scenic variety, and give sanctuary to animals and plants rarely seen on the mainland. In spite of Australia's extreme emphasis on seaboard settlement and maritime recreation, landing problems and a lack of fresh water saved many islands. Now an impressive number are fully protected as nature reserves. Others rank among our most celebrated national parks.

Remote island parks, with a controlled flow of visitors, are easily managed. But on closer islands – especially the Queensland islands with fringing coral – the risks of damage are high. The jeopardy of the reef at Green Island, off Cairns, prompted a marine park declaration. That concept of below-the-waterline protection is now applied in defence of almost all of the Great Barrier Reef region.

A scalloped beach line, seen strikingly at Safety Cove on Tasman Peninsula, Tas, results when incoming and receding waves collide and set up an eddying pattern. On a surfing beach, it may indicate dangerous rip currents

The Drum and Drumsticks, off Beecroft Peninsula, NSW, are remnants of an older coastline

THE NATURE OF AUSTRALIA

The eternal battle of the trees

PLANTS CANNOT RUN from hostile conditions. To survive, they must adapt and diversify. In Australia they have answered with an explosion of species. Flowering plants alone number about 11 000 kinds, from tiny herbs to towering eucalypts. Mosses, ferns, fungi and cone-bearing trees add to the array. And rivalry is intense. Plants struggle not only against climatic setbacks, animal appetites and human ambitions, but also against one another.

The story of land vegetation starts well over 400 million years ago. Leafless, branching strands of a mossy seaweed crept ashore from the intertidal zone and invaded swamps and marshes. Adapting to more and more exposure to the air, the plants evolved into mosses and colonised firm ground.

Root systems were developed to tap subsurface water. Plants with thick, rigid stems appeared – the ancestors of ferns, club-mosses and horsetails. Competing for light, they reached up on ever-stronger trunks and became the first trees. Forests grew widely, dominated by club-mosses 30 metres tall. Coal deposits are their petrified remains.

Next, more than 250 million years ago, came the conifers – pine trees and their relatives. They broke away from reliance on ground water to disperse reproductive spores; their pollen is produced high in the tree, to be scattered by winds. Another cone-bearing group, short-trunked cycads with palmlike or fernlike fronds, appeared at about the same time. Pines and cycads ruled until 80-90 million years ago.

Flowering plants were taking over by then, especially in warmer climates. Their vivid petals, alluring scents and nectar drew insects, ensuring a more effective transfer of pollen. Magnolias and figs were among the pioneers, and beeches gained early prominence in forests. Palms were soon abundant, and took many forms. The striking thing about the flowering plants was how quickly they produced variations to suit different soils and climates.

The realm of the conifers had been worldwide. But continental isolation was setting in when flowering plants came to the fore. Africa had separated from the southern supercontinent of Gondwanaland, and India and South America were in the process of breaking away. After New Zealand drifted off, about 80 million years ago, Australia's only neighbour – and source of new plants – was Antarctica.

In the last phase of separation, some 60 million years ago, southern Australia and Antarctica shared cool-climate rainforests. Conifers still predominated, among an increasing variety of flowering trees including some beeches. Almost nothing is known of the vegetation of inland and northern Australia, but it can be assumed that the forerunners of nearly all of today's species were established. The only important exceptions, in the far north, came much later from Asia through New Guinea.

Australia's breach with Antarctica was completed about 55 million years ago. The continent began its journey northwestward into warmer latitudes. But world temperatures generally were falling, and patterns of atmospheric circulation changing. Land upheavals and sea incursions modified climates and soils in the east and south. Browsing and grazing mammals and seed-eating birds spread. But plant evolution went on. Now in isolation, it took paths that were to create a uniquely Australian bush.

With the first uplift of the Eastern Highlands completed, about 45 million years ago, beech rainforests entered a long period of dominance

Pencil pine grows only in alpine Tasmania

BUILT BY PRIMITIVE PLANTS

CLUMPS like soft rock jut from sand and mud at Hamelin Pool, a shallow arm of Shark Bay, WA. In deeper water they stand in columns up to 3 metres tall. Found in thousands, these are living colonies of single-celled plants bound by secretions of lime.

The microscopic plants, called cyanophytes, represent the earliest form of life after bacteria – and the first to put oxygen into the air. They grow commonly in mats, like algae, and are usually grazed by molluscs. Only at Hamelin Pool are they left alone to build. The outlet is choked, and high evaporation makes the water too salty for molluscs.

Shorn-off cyanophyte mounds, solidified in silica, are found as big white rings in ancient rocks all over the world. Before their organic origin was known they were named stromatolites – 'mattress stones'. Some were built by plants growing 3000 million years ago.

Oddities of western and northern WA: Millstream palms (left) and baobabs or bottle trees – called boabs by locals

at least in the south. The general climate was still moist, but the interior of the continent was already more arid. And plants there were adapting. Trees that had emerged in luxury, enjoying abundant rainfall and rich soils, differentiated to include hardier forms.

Out of the acacia family – the wattles – came an exclusively Australian type with flattened, thornlike stems instead of leaves. From the myrtles, which in tropical America bear a soft, pulpy fruit, came eucalypts with tough, woody capsules. Both groups are thought to have gained some prominence in open forests by 30 million years ago. They and many other flowering trees continued to vary, developing scrubbier forms to survive in the poorest soils.

No one knows when the first alien plants may have arrived, their seeds carried by ocean currents or migratory birds. But intermittently over the past 10 million years, since Australia came into close contact with New Guinea, invaders of Southeast Asian origin have travelled overland. They established themselves with particular success in northern rainforests.

In most of the south, also about 10 million years ago, beech forests suddenly gave way to eucalypts. Some open woodlands and grasslands appeared, though their major expansion did not occur until 3-1 million years ago. By then the world was entering a period – continuing now – in which the climate fluctuated in cycles of glaciation and heating.

Trees advanced or retreated according to their resistance to frost, heat and drought – and increasingly to fire. Expanding populations of browsing animals chewed at them. Through it all, the grasses gained ground. They carpeted alpine plateaux and semi-arid plains, and clung in hummocks in places so barren that not even the scrub eucalypts and acacias could survive.

In a climate steadily more arid, rainforests

Cycads ruled for eons before palms evolved

were forced back to the eastern margins of the continent about 2 million years ago. Since then, in patches within those limits, they have contracted and expanded many times in a to-and-fro struggle with dry-adapted trees. And in tropical rainforests, the component plants have fought among themselves. Different species show up during each phase of resurgence, in fossils taken from the same spot.

Fire has been a powerful influence on Australian plant evolution for many millions of years. The fact that so many species benefit from burning and some even rely on it is evidence of that. But charcoal deposits and soil studies show a marked increase in the frequency of fires – and the expansion of grasslands – in the past 40 000 years.

Aborigines used fire to foster the wildlife they hunted. Blazes were started judiciously to keep woodlands clear of litter and encourage grass growth – not too often, yet not so seldom that huge conflagrations were caused. But European settlers anxious for agricultural land burned forests, woodlands and scrublands indiscriminately, and their raging fires bared far more ground than was needed.

Rainforest logging, the substitution of exotic plantations and the spread of introduced pasture grasses and farm crops have all had an obvious impact on native vegetation. More subtle is the conversion of soils by compaction under the hooves of thousands of millions of livestock. Often the bush is damaged by feral animals such as goats and pigs, or supplanted by alien trees and weeds. But on the vast scale of plant evolution, all these are just further complications – and perhaps passing phases – in a battle that never ends.

THE NATURE OF AUSTRALIA

Rainforests: a squandered heritage

Scores of tree species vie for space and light in the one small patch of tropical rainforest

RAINFORESTS are the scattered relics of an ancient time when most of Australia was moist and fertile. Driven back by a drying climate, they were overtaken by trees better able to resist drought and fire. Before Europeans came, the domain of rainforests was reduced already to less than 1 per cent of the continent's area. Now it is barely a quarter of that. In the main, whatever was most accessible has gone.

Generations of loggers and farmers who felled or burned the trees were largely ignorant of the consequences. They did not realise the extent to which they would trigger off soil erosion and the loss of water yields. They could not foresee a day when the forests would be needed to purify a polluted atmosphere. Least of all could they have understood that they were depleting a genetic store in which some stock – perhaps unseen – might be unique.

Even today it is not always grasped that rainforest species are interdependent. A certain tree may be widely distributed, so its removal from one forest seems harmless. But that could spell the doom of other plants whose habitat is more limited. Simply letting too much light in can kill many species. They may be merely fungi or mosses of no apparent significance. But they could have undiscovered properties important to human survival.

Shade – not just wetness or the types of trees – makes a rainforest. The leaves of the taller trees intermingle to form a canopy. By most botanical definitions, rainforests are at least 70 per cent enclosed under their canopies. Some are totally closed: treetops cannot be seen from the ground, and any light is filtered. Such forests are so humid that hot weather is intolerable – and so dark that walkers may be unable to see hazards.

Left alone, a rainforest recycles the mineral nutrients in dead trees and other fallen material. Decay is so rapid that the soil need not be especially fertile – nearly all the nutrients are stored above ground. But if erosion strips off the litter, or it is burnt and the ash washes away, the forest starves. So the local occurrence of rainforests is related not only to rainfall reliability but also to the least likelihood of fire. Even where eucalypts have come to rule, pockets of rainforest survive in protected gorges and gullies.

Tasmania has the most extensive rainforests – cool spreads of myrtle beech richly carpeted with mosses and ferns. They also occur in limited areas of Victoria. Stands of the closely related negrohead beech occupy high ranges in northern NSW and southern Queensland. Ancestors of these beeches were established before the southern supercontinent of Gondwanaland broke up: kindred trees grow in New Zealand and Chile and are fossilised in Antarctica. Later, beeches were probably the commonest forest trees in most of Australia.

Beech forests are simple in composition. Mature stands grow to a uniform height and have no understoreys made up of other tree species. Tree ferns may grow luxuriantly where the canopy is more open – particularly along riverbanks. But the forest floors are mainly mossy. Epiphytes – plants that attach themselves to others – and parasites, which feed off

Left: Cool-temperate forests of myrtle beech grow widely in Tasmania and in patches in Victoria – such as this one in Wilsons Promontory National Park. Tree ferns abound where the canopy opens along rivers

Negrohead beech, the ruler of temperate rainforests, nears the northern end of its range in Nightcap National Park, NSW

others, are few except for lichens. The beeches may grow to 30 metres, but in the coldest conditions do not exceed 10 metres.

Northern rainforests are much more complex. More than 100 different tree species may be found in one hectare, and none is noticeably dominant. The general height of the canopy is usually 30 metres or so, but here and there an emergent tree stands much taller. And below the canopy are understoreys of shorter trees. Vines climb towards the light, and epiphytes such as orchids and staghorn and elkhorn ferns are abundant. But the forest floor is surprisingly open. Palms and ferns grow fairly sparsely among fleshy-leafed herbs and a few small shrubs and tree seedlings. These seedlings seem never to get any taller – but if adult trees come down, through old age or storm damage, the opening of the canopy brings them shooting up to fill the gap.

Lichen-covered and nearly always buttressed at their bases, the different northern trees are hard to tell apart at ground level. Prized timber species surviving in remote forests include red cedar, coachwood, silky oak, Queensland maple and teak and the imposing kauri, which reaches 50 metres. This great pine, with relatives in New Zealand and New Caledonia, has a lineage even older than the beeches. The northern forests are equally a part of the Gondwanaland legacy.

Forests in the far north have been enriched more recently, however, by Asiatic plants arriving through New Guinea. That heightens a distinction often made between tropical and subtropical northern rainforests. The first kind contain many more species. But the division has nothing to do with the line of the Tropic of Capricorn – it relates to temperature ranges and altitude. Tropical forests in this sense are not found south of Townsville, and even to the north they are replaced by subtropical mixtures in the higher country.

The northern half of Cape York Peninsula has part-time rainforests. Plants here have to cope with months of drought between monsoons. So the forests are dominated by deciduous species that conserve moisture by shedding their leaves at the onset of the dry season. Since roads are open only in the 'Dry', most travellers do not recognise the rainforests. Small patches of similar vegetation occur in the Darwin region, where they are more often called monsoon vineforests.

Beyond their scenic value and their importance as botanical storehouses, rainforests are the busiest havens of wildlife on land. They seethe with the activities of myriads of creatures, at every level from the leaf litter to the topmost flower heads. Rare insects, amphibians, mammals and birds are among the occupants. Whatever threatens rainforests may ring the death knell of these animals.

Starting life as seeds lodged high in other tropical trees, curtain figs send down prop roots – then strangle their hosts

THE PARKS WHERE RAINFORESTS RULE

Pockets of rainforest are found in the majority of eastern national parks. Those parks where rainforest predominates, or takes up major areas, include:

Cairns region Barron Gorge, Bellenden Ker, Cape Tribulation, Clump Mountain (Maria Creek group), Daintree, Dunk Island, Ella Bay, Graham Range, Green Island, Grey Peaks, Iron Range, Lake Barrine, Lake Eacham, Lizard Island, Mount Hypipamee, Palmerston group, Topaz Road, Tully Gorge.

Townsville region Conway, Eungella, Goold Island (Hinchinbrook Island group), Jourama, Mount Jukes (Mount Blackwood group), Mount Spec, Orpheus Island, Wallaman Falls group, Whitsunday Island.

Rockhampton region Cape Palmerston, Coalstoun Lakes, Fairlies Knob (Mount Walsh group), Kroombit Tops, Mount Bauple, Northumberland Islands.

Brisbane region Bunya Mountains, Burleigh Head, Conondale, Lamington, Maiala (D'Aguilar Range group), Main Range, Natural Arch, Springbrook group, Tamborine Mountain group, The Palms.

NSW northern border region Border Ranges, Dorrigo, Gibraltar Range, Mount Warning, New England, Nightcap, Washpool.

Melbourne region Alfred, Tarra-Bulga, Croajingolong, Mitchell River, Otway, Wilsons Promontory.

Tasmania Cradle Mountain-Lake St Clair, Mount Field, Southwest, Walls of Jerusalem, Wild Rivers.

THE NATURE OF AUSTRALIA

The forests that welcome fire

Trees meet nature's harshest terms in Australia's open forests and woodlands. They face the certainty of wildfire. Many have adapted so that they can recover after burning. And some – particularly the eucalypts – now depend on fire for their procreation. They give typical 'gum tree' bushland not only its own look but even its own smell: evaporating oils.

Long before humans arrived to step up the pace of destruction, fires occurred naturally. Lightning strikes were most often the cause. The trees that stood the best chance were those with lignotubers – swellings near the base of the trunk containing latent buds. These come to life if the tree is damaged above. In some species lignotubers are seen as warty lumps on the trunk. But many Australian trees have them underground, extending much like roots.

Eucalypts and some of their companion trees in the open forests developed further defences. They enclosed their seeds in woody cases instead of soft fruits, and many acquired unusually thick bark. But the most successful species went beyond mere survival – they found ways of exploiting fire for their own benefit. They made sure that when a forest was burnt out, it was replaced by their offspring rather than an invading species. Evolution has brought some eucalypts to a point at which, once at least in their seed-bearing lives, they *need* burning down.

The tallest and fastest-growing eucalypts occupy high-rainfall districts. But they rely on strong light. If an overgrown forest becomes too shady, eucalypt seedlings are killed by fungi. Such a forest is waiting for a dry spell followed by a hot, fast-moving fire. Then, at the height of its destruction, it re-seeds itself.

Fed by streamers of peeling bark, flames race up the trunks to the forest canopy. Vaporised leaf oil ignites – sometimes it explodes – drawing the fire even more quickly away from the ground and through the canopy. And from under the vanishing foliage pours a shower of seed capsules – the output of not just one season, but perhaps three or four.

If the fire has moved on quickly enough the seeds are undamaged. (In a furnace test, green capsules protected their seeds for 9 minutes at 440°C.) Germination starts in a bed of ash, holding mineral nutrients in a form that the seedlings can most readily absorb. Their growth is astonishing: some saplings gain 5 metres in a year. In a burnt eucalypt forest, trees of other families have no chance of taking over.

Tall open forests – referred to in older books as wet hardleaf or wet sclerophyll forests – are at their most grand in the extreme southeast and southwest. In Tasmania and Victoria they include the world's tallest hardwood, mountain ash *Eucalyptus regnans*, which can exceed 100 metres. In Western Australia the karri *Eucalyptus diversicolor*, only slightly shorter, is king. Alpine ash, brown stringybark, blackbutt and blue gum are prominent in NSW, and rose gum is characteristic around Brisbane.

These forests are more open at the top than rainforests – canopy coverage is 30-70 per cent – but much leafier below. There is always a dense understorey of shorter eucalypt species and taller shrubs. On rich soils in the moistest areas, some of the understorey plants are rainforest species – on the way to taking over if fire does not come. With tree ferns, lichens and epiphytes abundant, some wet open forests at ground level look much like rainforests. But the trunk bases are not buttressed.

The dominion of eucalypts continues in drier open forests in southern Australia but the trees seldom exceed 30 metres. Fires are more frequent and most species are adapted to resist, then recover through lignotubers. Understoreys are less leafy, with acacias, casuarinas and banksias usually prominent. The most characteristic eucalypt species include peppermint, bloodwood, scribbly gum, stringybark and 'apple' (angophora) in the southeast, and

Heartwood fire dooms a tree – but its scattered seeds and underground tubers are intact

Damage higher up triggers new growth from a charred trunk

Left: A handsome stand of marri, with an understorey of karri oak, in WA's Walpole-Nornalup National Park. Marri grows widely in the southwest where it reaches heights of 30-40 metres. It shares the same range as jarrah and karri and often occurs with them. Its timber does not compare with that of the other two hardwoods – it is marred by gum pockets and rings

DIEBACK: SHARING THE BLAME

COUNTLESS diseases and pests attack eucalypts – especially where natural balances are disrupted. If large numbers of trees are slowly dying, their decline is generally labelled 'dieback'. It is not one problem but many, with different causes.

A soil-borne fungus attacks the giant jarrahs of Western Australia. To limit its spread some state forest areas and national parks are quarantined; there are wash-down facilities to prevent vehicles carrying infected soil from one area to another; road construction and use are restricted.

Dieback in irrigation areas (particularly in the Murray-Murrumbidgee Basin) occurs because of salting and an altered water table: too much water prevents soil aeration and rots tree roots; too little and the trees die of thirst.

Leaf-eating Christmas beetles and other insects are a major cause of eucalypt dieback in the New England district of NSW. Development of pastoral agriculture has provided more food for the beetles' larval stage while removing farmland trees so there are fewer birds to eat increasing numbers of beetles.

River red gum dieback in northwestern Victoria

In the Dandenong Ranges near Melbourne, the problem seems to be too many birds. Dieback has occurred in about 10 per cent of the forest cover because of an infestation by sap-sucking insects called psyllids. These are husbanded by a big population of bellbirds, which eat only the older psyllids and encourage the young to develop. Other birds with less selective appetites are driven away.

messmate, boxes and pink gum near Adelaide. The Perth region has its own group, dominated by jarrah, marri and wandoo.

Casuarinas and acacias rule in many open forests in Queensland, between hoop pine on the wetter seaward margins and cypress pine at the inland limit of forest growth. There are also some eucalypt forests, with grassy floors suggesting that they gained their hold through firing by Aboriginal hunters. Similar grassy eucalypt forests occur in the Darwin region and the Kimberleys, and along the Murray River Valley where they are dominated by the flood-loving river red gum.

Woodlands are distinguished from forests by having a canopy coverage of less than 30 per cent of their area. Often they are simply extensions of forest communities, more widely spaced because they have less soil moisture to share. Grasses are much more common, however. And some non-eucalypt species – melaleucas (paperbarks), for example – take on a prominence not seen in forests. Brigalow, once the most significant of woodland acacias, exists now only in remnants on its range from inland mid-Queensland to northern NSW.

In woodlands as much as in forests, eucalypts remain the most widespread and dominant trees. Their forms range from the snow gums of alpine summits to monsoon species that shed their leaves for the 'Dry'. Counting the stunted types of the outback, there may be more than 500 eucalypt species; botanists are forever making new finds and classifications,

Tree ferns are characteristic of the cooler wet eucalypt forests of the southeast – but never found in those of the west

and raising or lowering the figure. However many there are, eucalypts represent the plant kingdom's greatest evolutionary triumph – a conquest of every climatic extreme that the continent can offer.

But the unmistakable aroma of 'gum' leaves, and the blue haze pervading forests in hot weather, are reminders of menace. The layers of oily foliage and the thickly littered floors are incendiary bombs, certain sooner or later to go off. Eucalypts and many of their companions have accommodated to an element against which humans are largely helpless. Fire is a fact of their lives.

THE NATURE OF AUSTRALIA

Sentinels of the never-never

SCRUB, SPINIFEX and saltbush ... half of Australia is dismissed in three words. Yet in some ways the vegetation of the scorched, parched outback is the most important of all. It sustained the spread of Aboriginal tribes. It afforded the food, shelter and fuel to make the continent traversable – if seldom habitable – by Europeans and their livestock. And in spite of these intrusions, it has ensured the survival of many wildlife species.

Hardly any of the hinterland is absolute desert. Almost anywhere something grows, to make up the world's greatest array of dry-living plants. But two groups of stunted trees, mulga and mallee, have a hold so persistent that their habitats take their names. The Mulga is an immense tract of acacia scrub and sparse shrubland sweeping across Western Australia into the Northern Territory and South Australia, with outliers to the east. The Mallee's parched plains span southwestern NSW, northwestern Victoria and eastern South Australia. Even more mallee country extends west of Adelaide and round the Great Australian Bight to beyond Kalgoorlie, WA.

Mulga denotes one main wattle species, *Acacia aneura*, which on the best soils can reach 15 metres but in its shrub form can be as low as 2 metres. Its many branches, rising steeply from the ground or just above, carry slightly flattened stems – called phyllodes – instead of leaves. These have a hairy, resinous covering and point skyward to minimise heating. Trees go dormant in drought, but revive within four days of receiving moisture in their soil. They do best where there is some chance of rain at any time of year; in regions of strongly seasonal rainfall they tend to be replaced by casuarinas – the so-called oaks.

Aboriginal boomerangs and many souvenir ornaments are made of mulga wood. Livestock prefer browsing the phyllodes – though they are not particularly nutritious – to eating dry grass. Mulga is harvested as emergency fodder in droughts, and sometimes cleared where there is an understorey of edible tussock grasses. But the trees are secure in the driest areas, and where their understoreys are of inedible small shrubs or hummock grasses.

Mallees are ground-branching eucalypts. More than 100 species have been identified. They form a spreading bush, usually 3-9 metres tall, from an underground lignotuber that contains latent buds to regenerate the tree if it is damaged. Six months after a fire, they may have produced up to 70 new shoots. Stem branches are few and leaves are borne only at the tips of the branches. In dense scrub they form a distinctive canopy cover, shallow and almost horizontal.

Since drought-resistant wheat strains were developed, extensive mallee areas have been cleared – with some calamitous consequences. Without the cover of the mallees and their understorey shrubs and grasses, strong winds after long dry spells can rip all of the topsoil away. Millions of tonnes of red dust are dumped in choking storms on towns and cities or into the oceans; some is even blown as far as New Zealand.

On limy or salty soils, both mulga and mallee may merge into country dominated by low chenopod shrubs – saltbushes and their relatives. They are palatable to stock, and when agriculture invaded the outback their territories were the easiest to take. Saltbushes decline with years of grazing: of about 250 chenopod species, more than 20 are expected to disappear from the wild by the end of the century. But the others hold about 6 per cent of the mainland area. Most are in inland South Australia and on the Nullarbor Plain, with an isolated stronghold in western NSW around the dried-out Willandra Lakes.

Spiky hummock grasses dot arid land over a quarter of the continent, from the northwest coast into Queensland and south almost to the Nullarbor. Mostly species of *Triodia*, they are usually called spinifex – though true *Spinifex* exists as a coastal sand-binding plant. To avoid confusion some people call the inland hummock type porcupine grass. It normally occurs in mulga scrub or casuarina woodlands, but on rocky slopes and sandplains it may provide the only ground cover.

Open grasslands of softer, edible tussocks such as Mitchell grass range from south of Arnhem Land and the Gulf of Carpentaria to southwestern Queensland. But most are heavily grazed. Untouched grasslands now are vir-

Spinifex and snappy gums on the Hamersley Range, WA

Poached-egg daisies: the waiting is over

PLANTS THAT HIDE FROM DROUGHT

RAIN in late winter changes the look of arid inland regions with remarkable speed. Unseen in the ground are seeds that can bide their time through years of drought. When conditions favour them they burst into hectic life. Plants shoot in hours and flower in days. Almost as quickly they wither and die, leaving a new generation of seeds to wait once more.

Most such plants – called ephemerals – are members of the daisy or pea families. Their seeds are programmed so as not to be fooled by a passing shower, or by heavier rain at the wrong time of year. As well as searing heat, frost must be avoided. Germination is triggered only by a certain combination of moisture, temperature and light intensity.

Ephemerals have their easiest life near rock outcrops, where they may flourish annually in pockets of run-off moisture. In Central Australia, the seepage of dew from sealed, high-crowned highways is sometimes enough to promote growth along a narrow band at each side. But the most spectacular shows follow heavy rains on flat country. Drab tonings turn green, then explode into vivid colours as far as the eye can see.

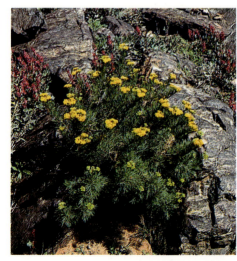

Hops and everlastings make the most of run-off

but most do not need to. Their seeds are distributed whenever they are ready – by harvester ants. These seeds all have a tough casing but they bear a soft tail. The ants carry the seeds to their nests, eat the tail, then discard the seeds undamaged. Sometimes they store them in underground galleries. Some 1500 Australian plant species use ants in this fashion, compared with fewer than 300 anywhere else in the world.

Heathlands in the east and south are generally small patches, merging into scrub or woodlands. Most are coastal, on sandy soils. But highland heaths occur in parts of the Great Dividing Range – on soils derived from sandstone or granite – and in Tasmania. In the west, immense tracts of heathland reach east from Albany and north from Kalbarri – not merely along the coast but also on sandplains well inland. It is their predominance that gives Western Australia its well-justified reputation as 'the wildflower state'.

Left: Mallees and pearl bluebush – a kind of saltbush – merge on the sandplains of Nullarbor National Park, SA. Feral camels are often seen

Below: Scrubs at Wyperfeld National Park, Vic, support at least 200 native bird species

tually confined to very wet areas – the high buttongrass plains of southwestern Tasmania, for example, or the swampgrass plains near parts of the NSW south coast.

Heathland plants make up the remainder of the vegetation of the wide-open spaces. In their domain, forest growth is ruled out not by aridity but by soil infertility. In compensation, the flowering shrubs of the heathlands present the most vivid scenes of the bush, and support a profusion of wildlife. Birds such as honeyeaters and parrots are likeliest to catch the eye, but smaller marsupials also feed on nectar and on the insects that swarm in the undergrowth.

Australia's main family of true heaths, the epacrids, has more than 300 species. The best known, common heath with its dangling tubular flowers borne year-round, is Victoria's floral emblem. Lilies and their relatives grow mostly as heath plants, along with thousands of smaller flowering species including ground orchids in a rich variety of forms and colours. But they and the true heaths are dominated by mixtures of taller woody shrubs. The most characteristic family, the proteaceae, includes banksias, grevilleas, hakeas, waratahs and Western Australia's dryandras. Small eucalypts, acacias, paperbarks, tea-trees and casuarinas are also common – but often the most distinctive plants of heathlands are grass trees.

Nearly all species on the fire-prone heathlands can regenerate from underground organs. Some release seed capsules during a fire,

PART TWO
Parks and people

Simple pleasures in a delightful setting: Walyunga National Park on the outskirts of Perth

Running a national park is a balancing act – protecting the environment while letting people enjoy it. Each place has its special problems, with dedicated rangers and backroom staff working to solve them. But a great deal more is up to the public.

PARKS AND PEOPLE

Why we have national parks

TAXPAYERS' MONEY goes into national parks, so people are entitled to see some return for it. Where parks provide recreational opportunities close to cities, or where they preserve unusually spectacular scenery, the benefits are clear. The value of protecting wildlife habitats is also widely recognised at last. But in an increasing number of cases, the worth of new parks is far from obvious to the public.

Some are dedicated in places that no one but a scientist would dream of visiting. Western Australia's vast Rudall River National Park, for example, covers a forbidding expanse of rock ridges and dunes between the Gibson and Great Sandy Deserts. It has no roads, and seldom any water. Many parks are sited in high country so rugged that it is penetrated only by expert climbers. Others occupy monotonous stretches of scrub or swampland, offering nothing noteworthy to see or do.

Public benefits are derived in indirect and sometimes unexpected ways. The real importance of a high, forested park may lie in ensuring the adequacy and purity of water supplies to a nearby community. Even without rain, trees shed more moisture than they receive from the air. And they combat air pollution.

Apart from the varying scenic and recreational merits of national parks, and their role in the protection of the environment and wildlife, they can offer four other advantages from which the whole community stands to gain:

Education Field studies by school groups and trainee teachers are given active assistance. Junior ranger programmes encourage children to follow nature interests in their spare time. Advice by parks staff is also offered in courses for private landowners.

Scientific research Professional studies and experiments are permitted in national parks if

Scientists are still exploring at Rudall River, WA. The public's turn will come much later

Schoolchildren find an easy introduction to nature study at Ferntree Gully National Park, Vic

they cannot be mounted elsewhere and are not unduly destructive. Untouched areas also serve as models, against which scientists can measure what happens when similar environments outside the parks are interfered with.

Biological banks Without park protection, many plants and animals would no longer exist. Their genetic combinations would be lost to the world. So would the possibility of using them to develop new medicines, food sources and industrial techniques.

Foreign income The fame of many of Australia's national parks is a powerful magnet to overseas visitors. And a major export earner, the fishing industry, depends on the protection of estuarine and island breeding grounds.

If planners had unlimited funds, they would provide many more parks. In the meantime, where population pressures are intense, they encourage passive recreation. They want visitors to relax, look and listen, rather than seek too many artificial amenities and active pastimes. Popular enjoyment has to be balanced against the fragility of natural environments – or else there may be nothing to enjoy later on.

Park administrations bear a responsibility to future generations, not only in Australia but also throughout the world. Our parks and wildlife services belong to an international union, formed under United Nations auspices, and the federal and state governments endorse all of its ideals. But we struggle to live up to them.

The international convention calls for national parks and nature reserves to make up at least 5 per cent of any country's territory. Australia, in spite of many recent additions, falls far short. And the parks are meant to represent every kind of biological community. Again Australia fails: virtually all temperate and subtropical grasslands, for example, have long been transformed by livestock.

Scarcity of land puts environmental aims in conflict with industrial interests. Remaining areas suitable for parks are often earmarked for mining or logging or hydro-electricity generation. Political pressures to continue industrial activity, at least for a time, are usually intense. Sometimes a mixture of uses seems entirely reasonable. But the international agreement requires a nation's 'highest competent authority' to eliminate any exploitation in national parks.

Australia's trouble has been that the highest authority, the federal government, holds absolute power only in Commonwealth territories – the ACT, the Northern Territory, Jervis Bay and some remote oceanic islands. Elsewhere, the federal system gives state governments the right to declare their own reserves and dispose of them as they please. Their older 'national' parks were created under diverse political influences to achieve different goals. Nationwide concerns were never paramount – let alone international responsibilities.

Dissension over such issues as uranium mining, oil prospecting and civil engineering continues to make political battlegrounds of some present and proposed national parks. But in management techniques and planning, at least, Canberra and the states are now in closer accord. Since the mid-1970s all legislatures have passed national parks and wildlife acts along broadly similar lines. Under a council of all the ministers with nature conservation responsibilities, senior officials of the various parks services form a standing committee to co-ordinate policies.

All of Australia's governments today have the benefit of the same high grade of professional advice on nature conservation, considered in the full light of national need. None of them wishes to be seen as environmentally irresponsible, so recommendations for new or expanded parks are usually received sympathetically. Whether enough money can be found to manage them, and provide the right balance of protection and public enjoyment, is altogether another matter.

The Royal: where it all started

Park expansion at Era took in holiday shacks – and herds of imported deer

IDEAS of nature conservation took a back seat in 1879, when Australia's first national park was conceived. The vision was not of a noble wilderness, to be kept sacred, but of a tamed and groomed playground – a Sydney version of London's Hampstead Heath.

Creation of the National Park (its only name for three-quarters of a century) was primarily a public health measure. Sydney's population had doubled in a decade: in some slums, one child in four died before it was five years old. The people needed common land.

Country to the south, cut off by the Hacking River, was about to be opened up by the Illawarra railway. Legislators reserved 7000 hectares for public recreation, and trustees hastened to meet the leisure tastes of the time. Riverside forest was hacked down to make way for lawns and European trees. Deer were brought in, and exotic birds and fish were released. A causeway controlled the river. Pavilions, guest houses and camps sprang up nearby. Cart roads and bridle paths wound into the bush. A tourist village, Audley, had its own vegetable plots, dairy pastures, orchard and blacksmith's forge.

Sports grounds were envisaged – even a horse racing track. In the meantime, undeveloped areas were cleared by the army for manoeuvres and artillery practice. And to recoup the cost of public amenities, the trustees were allowed to license grazing, logging and mining in the park.

Nature lovers were objecting before World War I, and in 1922 they successfully challenged a mining company's right to fell and mill native trees for pit props. But they could do nothing to stem the tide of cars that soon started to swamp the park. The trustees saw it as their duty to provide maximum access.

Motor roads criss-crossed the heathlands and reached the coastal cliffs and bays. People parked, picnicked, camped and cut firewood anywhere. Beach shacks appeared, and during the 1930s Depression the railway side of the park was dotted with humpies put up by jobless men. Some made livings by stealing greenery to supply city florists, or by selling cartloads of timber or soil.

Still more bush suffered in World War II, when the army set up coastal defences and used much of the park for training exercises. Postwar affluence brought a new flood of cars and motor bikes, and the first 'scrub bashers' in off-road vehicles.

The park was granted its Royal prefix in 1955, but to conservationists it seemed a lost cause. Still, it served as an object lesson, readily pointed to by professional ecologists when official policies came under fire in the next decade. After NSW set up Australia's first integrated parks and wildlife service in 1967, the professionals took charge of the mutilated old reserve and set about giving it another chance.

Cars were restricted to a few formed roads and parking zones. Ramshackle buildings were demolished. Maintenance of ornamental gardens and any other attempts to outdo nature were abandoned. The bush came back, season by season, until in its centenary year at the end of the 1970s the Royal National Park could wear its title with some pride.

Imitating an English pleasure garden suited Sydney ideas of ease in Edwardian times

Soldiers took over in World War I, baring the heathlands

PARKS AND PEOPLE
Jacks and Jills of all trades

OUTDOOR WORK in a pleasant setting... that is one part of the picture of a park ranger's life. But another may be writing reports and keeping financial records – or cleaning lavatories. Some tasks entail days and nights of utter solitude. Others require the poise and patience to deal with constant streams of people. Physical demands are high. Rangers have to be dedicated, fit and above all versatile.

Looking after the public constitutes the major part of the workload. Visitors expect easy road access and parking. They want eating facilities, campsites, piped water and sanitation – and nobody else's garbage. They seek information: signposts, leaflets, displays, advice. And they are entitled to safety. Walking routes must be secured and waterways patrolled. People astray in big parks may have to be found and helped, and perhaps given first-aid treatment. But all too often, what park visitors need most is policing.

Enforcement of regulations is the priority role of all rangers. They must keep dogs, cats and firearms out of parks, and make sure that no native plants, animals, rocks or soil are taken without licence. They must try to prevent off-road driving, and any intrusion into areas that are quarantined because plants are regenerating or endangered animals are breeding. Vitally, they have to see that fire restrictions and bans are obeyed.

Every year the parks services report hundreds of prosecutions and fines. Many other infringements are dealt with by a formal caution or just a friendly reminder – sometimes at the risk of abuse or violence. A Sydney Harbour ranger, patrolling by launch, spotted a beach party round an illicit fire. He went ashore to chide the group and was brutally bashed. Even organised crime impinges on parks: rangers in remote districts have had tense encounters with drug smugglers and marijuana growers.

Practical work to protect the environment is often sheer hard labour. Firebreaks and trails have to be maintained, and precautionary burns carried out. Most parks are at constant war with noxious weeds, feral animals or soil and sand dune erosion. Many have vandalism to contend with as well, or simply the inevitable wear and tear of heavy visiting. And parks services are increasingly taking over and trying to restore land damaged by other uses.

Rangers' reports form the basis of much of the park information that is distributed to the public. They also contribute to the resource studies and environmental impact assessments that precede major changes in management policies. Rangers may be called on for field observations to establish the numbers and movements of endangered animals, the location of rare plants, or the rate of decay of delicate landforms. Their judgments help decide where visitors are encouraged to go and what they are encouraged to do.

Educating the public is another big role. Some rangers spend much of their time running information and display centres or conducting guided walks. School parties receive special treatment, and rangers also go to schools for classroom talks. Landholders are offered advice on soil conservation, native tree care, wildlife protection, pest control and so on. Public relations addresses are often made to community groups – including some that are opposed to national parks. Hardest to win over are farmers who fear crop raids by animals from nearby parks, local body leaders who resent the loss of ratable land, and people whose livings depend on logging or mining.

Rangers of both sexes are highly trained in emergency procedures: fire fighting, search and rescue, first aid and sometimes flood response. Often they trap or kill animals – in the far north, their tasks may include buffalo musters and crocodile shoots. But little of a ranger's work is so exciting. Much more is mundane: fixing, cleaning and improving facilities, removing refuse, spraying weeds, supervising and informing visitors, issuing permits, collecting fees, answering mail and attending to clerical details.

Many ranger tasks are sheer drudgery: emptying garbage bins is not the worst of them

Carpentry skills ease a climb for nature trail parties

Winter duties in the Victorian Alps include clearing away snowdrifts so that skiers can get to their slopes – and then retrieving casualties

While tourists shun Kakadu's 'Wet', hard work goes on

THE POWER BEHIND THE PATCH

EMBLEMS patched on every park ranger's uniform are symbols of helpfulness and protection – and firm authority if it is needed. In enforcing certain laws on behalf of their state or territorial services, rangers have powers similar to those of the police. They carry identity cards stating their role as park wardens: their instructions must be obeyed.

Prosecutions for minor breaches of park rules are rare, but offenders who interfere with other people's enjoyment can be evicted. Formal letters of warning may be issued, so a ranger is entitled to ask for a culprit's name and address. To refuse is a further offence.

Under the laws that protect native plants and animals in parks, rangers acting on reasonable suspicion can search vehicles, containers and camps, seize any flora or fauna, and confiscate firearms and other hunting gear. In states where park rangers are also wildlife officers – not Victoria or Western Australia – their powers of search and seizure can extend to private property outside a park.

Positions are so sought after, however, that the parks services can be extremely selective. They usually insist on land management experience, and some states require applicants to hold a diploma in park management, environmental studies or natural sciences. And even that does not guarantee them a job – let alone any choice in where they work. Some busy parks employ a less formally qualified grade of 'park worker', chosen usually for manual skills. But the rangers themselves are expected to be competent and self-reliant in work such as carpentry and mechanical maintenance, along with bushcraft.

Staff with the highest qualifications usually work from regional centres or state head offices. They include architects, designers, lawyers, archeologists and publications specialists. But most are science graduates and technicians, conducting biological and environmental research. A few in each state concentrate on interpretation – the evaluation and explanation of park resources – and planning. This provides the main basis of management policy, which in turn determines how the rangers in the field have to do their work.

Queensland rangers collect data for turtle research

PARKS AND PEOPLE

Staying alive in the bush

FIRE IS BY FAR the greatest danger that visitors could face in national parks. When hot winds blow, bushfires can flare with little warning and approach with astonishing speed. But they move on just as quickly. Applying some commonsense safety procedures, no one need be killed or even badly burnt.

In the first place, parks consisting of eucalypt forests, dense scrub or heavily vegetated heathlands are best avoided when fire risks are extreme. They will be stiflingly hot and dusty anyway – hardly enjoyable unless they give access to rivers. Most parks display risk indicators near their entrances. And on the worst days, when total fire bans are declared, they are announced in all radio, newspaper and television weather reports. Check before setting out for a park; if there is a total ban in the district, consider changing your plans.

Fire bans are declared by statewide authorities. But park managements at any time can impose their own rules on the types of fires allowed. These are made clear on signs and in leaflets. Whichever sort of restriction applies, it is enforceable in court. Ignoring it could cost a stiff fine – even jail – or people's lives. For safety's sake alone the rules must be obeyed. And smokers have a particular responsibility to see that matches and butts are extinguished.

The killer in bushfires is not usually flame,

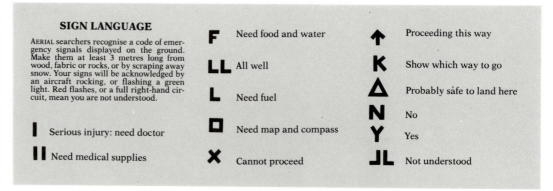

SIGN LANGUAGE

AERIAL searchers recognise a code of emergency signals displayed on the ground. Make them at least 3 metres long from wood, fabric or rocks, or by scraping away snow. Your signs will be acknowledged by an aircraft rocking, or flashing a green light. Red flashes, or a full right-hand circuit, mean you are not understood.

- **I** Serious injury: need doctor
- **II** Need medical supplies
- **F** Need food and water
- **LL** All well
- **L** Need fuel
- **☐** Need map and compass
- **X** Cannot proceed
- **↑** Proceeding this way
- **K** Show which way to go
- **△** Probably safe to land here
- **N** No
- **Y** Yes
- **⌐⌐** Not understood

but radiated heat. Shield yourself from it. If you are on foot with a fire approaching, don't flee blindly. Look around for the best refuge – in a steep-banked creekbed, or behind a rock outcrop or a fallen log where the vegetation is thinnest. Keep low as you move – crawl if you must – to avoid smoke inhalation. If there is no shelter in sight, lie face down on a bare patch of ground. Scoop out a hollow for yourself if you can, and use loose soil to cover any exposed skin. When the main blaze has passed over you, move to where nothing is left to burn.

If you are in a car, stay there – it is your best possible shield against radiant heat. Cars are unlikely to catch fire, and sealed petrol tanks do not explode. Never try to drive through smoke. Park at the roadside – avoiding thick undergrowth and long grass – and turn on your headlights. Close windows and air vents, and block any chinks with paper or fabric. Get down on the floor and use the mats to cover exposed skin.

Bites and stings Never walk far into the bush without long trousers, socks and thick footwear. Take the greatest care where you tread on warm, sunny days, when snakes are most active. If you see a snake in your path, don't try to poke at it – annoyed in that way, it is most likely to strike. But if you stand well clear and make plenty of noise, it will go away.

Most of Australia's 140 snake species are venomous, but only about 15 are capable of killing humans. Unless you are expert in identifying species, however, regard any snakebite as dangerous. Apply a bandage that puts firm pressure *directly on the bitten area* – not a tourniquet. If a limb is bitten, immobilise it with a splint. Then quickly alert a ranger. The park may have its own venom-identification kit and anti-venom supplies.

A lethal species of funnel-web spider (*Atrax robustus*) is a threat to life only in the Sydney region. It is black and big – up to 7 cm across between leg-tips. Treat a funnel-web bite like a snakebite, with pressure bandaging and immobilisation. One other dangerous spider, the redback, may be found anywhere in Australia. Dark, with an orange-red stripe on its back, and measuring 2-3 cm across, its venom is slower-acting and bandaging is unnecessary if medical aid can be obtained quickly.

Bush ticks abound in eastern forests. Tiny when they attach themselves, they burrow into the skin and feed on blood for three or four days, swelling to about 1 cm across. Meanwhile they release a paralysing toxin that can lead to death, especially in children. If you have brushed through dense vegetation, inspect exposed areas of skin for the next three days – and have someone else examine your scalp. A lightly attached tick may be scraped off. One

Rangers and police practise rescue techniques in the Labyrinth at Cradle Mountain-Lake St Clair, Tas

BURNING WITH A PURPOSE

TASMANIAN rangers (pictured below) in Southwest National Park are lighting their own bushfire. It will turn hundreds of hectares into a blackened waste. But these men are making sure that a worse fire will not happen by accident.

The disaster potential of bushfires depends largely on how much fuel they can find. Preventive burning in national parks is ordered before the build-up of litter and undergrowth reaches a dangerous level. Not only the quantity of fuel but also its composition, distribution and moisture content are calculated – in some places with computers.

Frequent burning around the edges of parks is normally done by hand, but bigger tracts inside are more often fired with air-dropped incendiary capsules. Under most fire management programmes, only small sections of each park have to be burnt and closed off for regeneration. In the southeast, for example, preventive burning of as little as 5 per cent each year is enough to keep a whole area safe from full-scale destruction.

embedded more deeply can be killed with kerosene or turpentine, and perhaps prised out with tweezers. If this is not wholly successful, seek medical help. Leeches, which are bigger and less likely to escape notice in the first place, are seldom harmful. They drop out after about five minutes of feeding, or if killed with a burning cigarette end or twig. Don't pull them out – parts left in may cause an infection.

Big, aggressive saltwater crocodiles are increasing in some tropical parks. Remember, they are just as much at home in fresh water. Observe signs warning against swimming and take special care walking on riverbanks. If you find yourself near a basking crocodile, back off quietly. Never place yourself in its path to the water. It may use its tail to knock you out of the way – and one blow from a fullgrown 'saltie' could kill you.

Safety first Unless you are a fit and fully experienced bushwalker, stick to established paths and trails. Don't attempt a long journey through rugged or untracked country unless you have a party of at least three – then if someone is in trouble, another can stand by while the third goes for help. Always carry more water than you believe you will need, along with a first-aid kit and a compass, whistle, knife and waterproof matches. Don't start without obtaining up-to-date maps and telling a ranger of your intentions. And don't fail to report back when the trip is over, if you are asked to. Your negligence could spark a wasteful search operation.

If you are lost, assess your food and water supplies and ration them. Don't waste energy by moving about aimlessly. Seek shelter near an open space where signals can be seen from aircraft, and stay put. If you are forced to keep moving, leave messages along your route or mark it in some way, indicating your direction. To attract attention if other people seem to be nearby, give three whistles, shouts or mirror-flashes at regular intervals, and light a smoky fire of leaves or grass.

Fire-watching from the summit of Mt Lofty becomes a fulltime job during danger periods at Cleland Conservation Park, near Adelaide. Below: Backburning to contain a fast-moving wildfire

PARKS AND PEOPLE
How the public can help

IF YOU WOULD enjoy using some spare time to help maintain and improve a favourite national park, just ask. Almost certainly you will be put in touch with a band of volunteers already in action in the district. Most parks – especially those near major population centres – have arrangements with outside groups.

Hundreds of Australians find agreeable fresh-air exercise in voluntary park work at weekends and during holidays. There is room for more. Many tasks are menial: litter removal, weeding and tree planting are typical. But other jobs are highly constructive and add significantly to park amenities. Some are funded by community service clubs and business organisations.

Rapid volunteer response is credited with saving major parts of parks threatened by severe erosion after storm damage. Others, devastated by fire or flooding, have been brought back into public use surprisingly quickly thanks to donated labour. Sometimes a task is long overdue, but simply too hard for the park service to justify on a limited budget. 'Friends of the Prom', for example, trekked back and forth between Melbourne and Wilsons Promontory National Park to remove decades of painted graffiti from rocks at Refuge Cove.

Volunteers with manual trade skills, or experience in plant care on a large scale, are usually most welcome. Others who are adept at dealing with visitors, and can acquire the knowledge to interpret a park's natural fea-

Queensland volunteers pitch in to clear a trail

tures and answer questions, may be enlisted at busy times to help at information centres or take parties on guided walks.

The Australian Trust for Conservation Volunteers, originating in Victoria but spreading nationwide in 1984, offers mobile squads of young people for national park assignments. These task forces usually camp on the site. Their first big accomplishment, in 1982, was the construction of 4.5 km of rabbit fencing at Hattah-Kulkyne National Park. Since then they have restored jetties, improved tracks, built footbridges and eradicated noxious weeds at various parks – and even cleaned up a disused guesthouse to accommodate visitors.

Members of the public are also entitled to have their say in the planning of national parks – where they should be and what activities should be allowed in them. Management plans are published, and in some states and the ACT the law demands that public comment be invited. Even without such a provision, there is nothing to stop an interested citizen making representations to the appropriate parks service or environment department. A sympathetic MP would probably give assistance.

But individuals have a hard time making themselves heard on national parks issues. Most arguments are too technical, resting on resource evaluations and environmental impact assessments. People seeking to sway government or park management decisions are advised to consult one of the National Parks Associations or a similar organisation.

ORGANISATIONS YOU CAN JOIN

PUBLIC organisations in every state and territory work for the establishment of new national parks, and generally to see that natural environments are not only conserved but also enjoyed.

National Parks Associations, which advance detailed cases to governments for the creation of new parks, are based in Sydney, Melbourne, Brisbane and Canberra. Equivalent bodies elsewhere are the SA Nature Conservation Society (Adelaide), the WA Conservation Council (Perth), the Tasmanian Conservation Trust (Hobart) and the NT Environment Council (Darwin).

National Parks and Wildlife Foundations, which conduct fund-raising appeals – such as NSW's annual 'Operation Noah' – to help acquire land for parks and conserve endangered animals, are based in Sydney and Adelaide. The **Australian Conservation Foundation,** with headquarters in Melbourne, focuses attention on wider environmental issues at a national level, but gives particular support to the national parks movement.

National Trusts, besides their work to save items of cultural heritage such as historic buildings, are active in promoting nature conservation. They have offices in all capital cities. The **Wilderness Society,** having triumphed in its No Dams campaign in Tasmania, has set up branches in nearly all mainland capitals.

World Wildlife Fund Australia, based in Sydney, raises money to preserve endangered species in Australia and some nearby Pacific islands. **Environment Centres** in all capitals and in many provincial cities provide public information and administrative facilities for the environmental movement as a whole. They can give you details of hundreds of other local and special-interest groups that may suit your purpose.

NOTE: Addresses at back of book

Outside helpers remove thorn apple, a noxious weed, from a creekbed in Snowy River National Park, Vic

Making the most of your visit

CREATION of a national park is no guarantee of stunning scenery or exciting activities. Australia's 500-odd parks are meant to preserve widely different environments. Not all may be to your liking. Many will lack the facilities to meet your particular needs. So in planning a visit, make sure you know what to expect.

From information in the regional guide sections that follow, readers can decide for themselves which parks are likely to hold most attraction and how much time they want to spend in them. Descriptions are down to earth – not glamorised. And the interest ratings are equally realistic. If a park rates low in 'day activities', for example, it means there is little to do but look around. There may not be enough to keep children amused for long.

In arranging a tourist itinerary, check on the availability of campsites. If you are interested in visiting several parks it may not be necessary to contact them all in advance – the capital city head office of the National Parks Service should be able to warn you of any difficulty. Queensland has a tourist pre-booking system, operated from Brisbane and regional offices, that covers all of its camping parks.

Consider the time of year and the weather, especially if a long journey outside your home district is involved. Most parks in the tropics, and many others inland, are far from enjoyable in summer. In the bushfire season, or if there have been heavy rains, call the enquiries number before setting out, to make sure that the park of your choice is open and accessible.

If you are travelling with a dog or cat, remember that you cannot take it into a national park. The menace that an escaped cat presents to wildlife is obvious. Few dogs are such efficient hunters – but their mere barking is enough to terrify native animals and disrupt their living patterns for days afterwards.

When you arrive at a park, or at a town office that looks after camping permits, pick up all the explanatory material offered. Anything that heightens your powers of observation will increase your enjoyment. And without full information, you may miss major points of interest. Nearly all parks have general maps. Some have leaflets to aid in bird spotting and plant identification, and special maps for bushwalks and self-guiding nature trails.

Public roads are kept to a minimum in all parks. Be prepared to leave your car in a designated parking area – never drive it into the bush – and see the sights on foot. It is by far the best way. Leaflets or signposts will tell you how long a walk should take, and whether it presents any difficulty.

Knowledge adds interest: an excellent example of park literature from the Northern Territory

WILDLIFE

The numbat, a rare termite eater, is protected at Dryandra Forest, WA

Scientists are intrigued by Eungella's gastric-brooding frog

Where animals

WERRIKIMBE National Park gained an extra 20 000 hectares of rainforest in 1984 – all for the sake of some mice. They are of a native species found in significant numbers only two years before. Now their home, on the upper Hastings River in northern NSW, should be secure.

Queensland has dedicated one of its national parks solely to preserve the habitat of an endangered species. The northern hairy-nosed wombat survives only at Epping Forest – formerly part of a cattle station on flat, semi-arid woodland west of Gladstone. Fencing keeps out grazing livestock and allows the regeneration of native grasses and scrub on which the wombat colony depends.

Successful husbandry of rare animals – especially those newly discovered – relies on complicated biological research and the scientific monitoring of populations and feeding habits. Only the national parks and wildlife services have the specialised resources for such work, so most conservation efforts are centred on their parks, or on some state parks under their management. Forestry and water catchment authorities play important co-operative roles.

A recent triumph of wildlife conservation has been the saving of the malleefowl in Victoria. It is the world's only mound-nesting bird living in arid regions. Clearing and grazing of its scrub habitats, along with bushfires, had all but wiped it out by the 1950s. But populations flourish

Parks were specially dedicated to rescue the endangered malleefowl. The male spends 8 months every year building a mound in which eggs are buried

Right: Only Kakadu, NT, has Leichhardt's grasshopper

For half a century the Hastings River mouse was known only from English museum specimens. Now it has a park section all to itself, where researchers are trying to discover its habits

find safety

Iron Range, Qld, is a haven for the golden-shouldered parrot

Left: A Queensland ranger examines a ghost bat — our only carnivorous species. Big colonies are seen at Fitzroy Caves and nearby Mt Etna

now in Little Desert, Hattah-Kulkyne and Wyperfeld National Parks. Mallee Cliffs National Park, in far western NSW, was established with the same aim.

Judging whether a species is truly rare can be difficult in Australia. Much of the fauna is small, secretive and nocturnal in habit. It is hard to find, let alone to count. And fires, floods and prolonged droughts lead to drastic fluctuations in numbers and distribution.

A highly unusual frog, discovered in 1972, disappeared after 1979. It lived in Kondalilla National Park and the neighbouring Conondale and Blackall Ranges of southeastern Queensland. Called the platypus frog because of its swimming action, it seemed to be the only frog in the world that never left water. And it was the world's only known gastric-brooding vertebrate. Females swallowed fertilised eggs and raised their young in their stomachs — somehow shutting off the production of digestive acids.

Rediscovery was hailed in 1983, when similar orange-coloured gastric-brooders were spotted far to the north in Finch Hatton Gorge, which leads out of Eungella National Park. But a captured specimen, compared with one of the Kondalilla frogs still alive in an Adelaide laboratory, proved to belong to yet another new species. The likelihood of other finds offers medical researchers high hopes of developing a drug to prevent human stomach ulcers.

The task of tallying animal populations is full of such surprises. Camping out in 1982 to count waterfowl, a wildlife officer in northwestern Tasmania made a convincing observation of a thylacine, or marsupial 'tiger'. Most people thought the species was extinct. But this animal's doglike head and black-striped, tawny back were unmistakable. Word of the sighting was withheld from the public for two years. If the breeding grounds of thylacines are traced, they will receive the strictest protection ever known.

Skunk-like in its markings, the striped possum of tropical rainforest parks is also remarkably smelly

RESTORATION

Nature gets another chance

WOUNDED LANDSCAPES are hard to heal. Even where full restoration is possible, the cost is often prohibitive. But national parks staff are succeeding, here and there, in turning back the clock. Their techniques were largely developed in old-established parks degraded by decades of heavy visiting. Now they are applied to recently resumed land that has suffered from other uses.

Most new inland parks have been at least partly grazed by livestock. The effect on natural vegetation is compounded by the persistence of feral animals – species that were introduced as domestic stock but now breed in the wild. Goats and pigs do the most widespread damage. Wild rabbits still bare the land in some districts, in spite of the sweeping eradication measures of the 1950s. High-country parks are often scarred by old logging trails or forestry roads, their margins invaded by exotic weeds. Steeper slopes may be subject to soil erosion.

When coastal parks are acquired, they frequently come with a legacy of dune erosion from off-road vehicles and ill-placed walking tracks. Many include old sand mining leases, or quarries where lime or building stone were extracted. Before the usual chores of removing noxious weeds and planting sand-binding grasses can start, the original land contours may have to be rebuilt.

Some park areas have a history of military use. They were taken over still bearing the marks of bombing or artillery practice and infantry exercises. Among the latest acquisitions are the various high headlands that make up most of Sydney Harbour National Park. These would not be available to the public now – suburban housing would have enveloped them – if they had not been reserved for 150 years or more as defence posts. Vantage points are capped with gun emplacements; the sandstone below is riddled with ammunition chambers, snipers' slits and connecting tunnels. The fortifications are worth keeping for their historical value – but their bare surroundings, stripped of soil by wind erosion, were an eyesore. Years of work and substantial funds are going into restoration

Sand mining roads scar a proposed park extension on Nth Stradbroke Island, Qld

Right: Regeneration of grazed land on Bogong High Plains, Vic, is a co-operative venture

A goat is fitted with a radio collar to track its movements

of the heaths and woodlands that greeted the First Fleet.

Bush regeneration calls for fine judgment, skilled work and inexhaustible patience. Attempts to make dramatic improvements overnight, simply by ripping out alien weeds or dumping new topsoil, are bound to fail. The same weeds – if not worse ones that are even faster-growing – will reappear, and probably work their way deeper into any natural bush nearby. Only a cautious approach, aimed at tipping the balance subtly towards native plants, is likely to succeed.

Managed regeneration of weed-infested bush starts from the least affected area and works towards the most degraded. In weeding, the soil is disturbed as little as possible and surface mulch is put back in place so that any native seeds lie at the proper level. The pace of progress is dictated by the capacity of seedlings to reclaim territory. They must have time to form a dense, diverse community in one zone – and planners must be convinced that it can be kept clear of weeds – before a neighbouring area is touched.

In rainforests the process is complicated by the interaction of plants. The different growth habits of weeds have to be considered, so that they are taken out in the correct order. If tall, leafy vines are removed first, for example, stronger light reaching the forest floor may spur the spread of ground creepers that choke off native seedling growth. Extensive regeneration projects, whether of rainforest trees or of eucalypts and their companions, take many years.

Control of feral animals calls for just as much patience. Little is achieved without a thorough knowledge of how they live in particular habitats. The breeding rate of a species may vary from place to place, depending mainly on climate and the availability of food. Patterns of movement also vary. Some plants and land are more easily damaged than others. All these factors influence a decision on how much control – which usually means killing – is necessary in a park, and what method will work best.

Wildlife suffers heavily from predation by feral cats and dogs and dingoes, and from the competition these and other species create for food, water and shelter. Rabbits and goats strip any vegetation they can reach

THE SCOURGE OF NATIVE WILDLIFE

CATS breeding in the wild are the most efficient of all predators. Their chief impact is on native birds, small mammals and reptiles. Indirectly they can also upset plant life, because they eat many of the animals that control insect pests.

Nearly all feral cats revert to a tabby appearance. Most are greyish, but on red outback soils more are ginger. In forested regions, where food is easily obtained, they are heavier than domestic cats but not noticeably bigger.

But in harsher country, it is survival of the fittest. The most powerful cats get the food – and the biggest toms take all the breeding opportunities. Supercats are evolving. Some stand twice as tall as their ancestors and are many times heavier. One giant shot in the Simpson Desert weighed 12 kg.

above ground, and pigs do even worse – they root into the soil with their snouts and leave it fit for nothing but weeds. Water buffalo in the Northern Territory trample and degrade wetlands that are important to tourism and vital to migratory waterfowl. And many feral species are potential carriers of exotic livestock diseases – tuberculosis and brucellosis, for example – that in uncontrolled conditions could be ruinous to the agricultural economy. In their extermination measures, parks services work in close co-operation with farming communities.

Feral pigs lay waste a waterhole at Kinchega, NSW

Trees return to former farmland at Organ Pipes, Vic

41

Heritage list

Mt Lidgbird on Lord Howe Island rises 777 metres from the edge of a coral-encrusted lagoon. The Lord Howe group, 700 km northeast of Sydney, is regarded as an outstanding example of an island system developed from submarine volcanic activity. Many of its plants and animals are found nowhere else. Much of the main island is protected under NSW national parks and wildlife laws as a 'permanent park'

Below: Forests crowd the deep gorge of the Franklin River in Wild Rivers National Park. This park forms the centre of the western Tasmanian World Heritage area, together with the neighbouring Southwest and Cradle Mountain-Lake St Clair National Parks

An obligation

NATURAL FEATURES of Australia figure importantly as World Heritage sites. Already listed are the Great Barrier Reef, Kakadu National Park, western Tasmania's chain of wilderness parks, the Willandra Lakes region of NSW, the Lord Howe Island group, and the rainforest parks and reserves of northern NSW. Uluru National Park, embracing Ayers Rock, is expected to be added.

Some great national parks overseas, such as Grand Canyon and Yellowstone in the USA, are among the nearly 200 other 'properties' on the list. But the majority are sites of ancient civilisations, or manmade structures of cultural importance. They include many famous cathedrals and palaces — along with the infamous Auschwitz concentration camp.

Inclusion of a natural area is a source of pride to any country. It confers recognition that the area is of world significance because it: represents a major stage of the

THE ANCIENT ROCK ART OF KAKADU
ABORIGINAL sites in Kakadu National Park, occupied for at least 25 000 years, include rock galleries of elaborate prehistoric paintings. Pictured are two from the hundreds seen by visitors to Ubirr (Obiri Rock).

Sand lunettes, windblown from the beds of the dried-up Willandra Lakes, hold evidence of human activity more than 30 000 years ago

to the world

earth's evolution; exemplifies continuing geological processes, biological evolution and human interaction with the environment; contains rare or superlative natural features or areas of exceptional beauty; or supports rare or endangered plants and animals.

But along with pride goes a heavy obligation. When a site is nominated for World Heritage listing, the nation responsible undertakes to ensure 'identification, protection, conservation, presentation and transmission to future generations ... to the utmost of its own resources'. The nominating nation is also obliged to obtain international assistance if it is needed to achieve those aims.

Some loss of sovereignty and secrecy is implied. That may be why the world list is noticeably incomplete: China and the Soviet Union have nothing on it. And in Australia's case the commitment made by the federal government clearly overrides states' rights. That was established in the High Court over the Tasmanian dam argument.

Australia's nominations are proposed by the Australian Heritage Commission. Its chairman and six members are part-timers appointed by the federal Environment Minister and drawn from a variety of professions in all states. They also supervise the selection and documentation of other important natural or cultural sites in Australia, and the compilation of a register of what is called the National Estate. Fraser Island, when it was rescued from sand mining, became the inaugural entry on that local list.

World Heritage nominations are received at UNESCO headquarters in Paris. Seventy countries have signed the convention that governs the listing procedure. Nominations go before a committee of 21 national representatives, with a membership that changes frequently so that every country gets a turn. The committee meets to approve listings towards the end of each year.

The Great Barrier Reef is the biggest Heritage area of all

PART THREE
A guide to the national parks of South Australia, Victoria & Tasmania

Parks are grouped on the basis of their accessibility from major population centres and their proximity to one another. In each region a pictorial selection is followed by a directory of parks. It gives their location, indicates their character and identifies the public facilities they offer.

Comparative ratings, assessed by parks staff, are aimed at helping visitors decide on the destinations that will give them most satisfaction. As a further aid, the activities allowed in national parks are listed along with the parks in which they may be pursued.

Nullarbor National Park, South Australia

ADELAIDE REGION

Where an artist found wonder in wastelands

SETTLERS from Britain were slow to see any beauty in sun-scorched, dusty lands and lonely eucalypts. They signified hardship and despair. But early this century a German-born painter opened Australian eyes. Working mainly in the Flinders Ranges, Hans Heysen mastered the intensity of light in the dry outback, catching contrasts of form and tone in watercolours of haunting power.

He is remembered fittingly in the Heysen Trail, now being developed by the South Australian government. A system of connected walking and horse-riding tracks will reach from the northernmost heights of the Flinders to the ocean shores of Fleurieu Peninsula. Sections completed, spanning about 500 km, take in the state's best-known inland parks – including the scraps of forest that survive on the Mt Lofty Ranges just east of Adelaide.

Densely wooded country is rare in this generally semi-arid climate. The raised plain and steep scarps of the Mt Lofties catch just enough winter rain. But land reserved here, so close to the capital, suffered heavily from recreational use. Under strict international principles adopted in the early 1970s, some old national parks were stripped of their status. Many such areas are now called conservation parks – a designation that means priority is given to the conservation of wildlife and plants and preservation of the natural landscape. Some conservation parks, such as Cleland, Black Hill, Seal Bay, Naracoorte and Deep Creek, have good visitor facilities. When restored to a more natural condition, enlarged and with extra amenities, they may emerge as national parks.

Away from the ranges, parks within easy reach of Adelaide are chiefly appreciated for their coastal scenery and the maritime activities they allow – especially fishing. Their sparse vegetation may be less appealing, but it provides habitats for a surprising diversity of wildlife. Adelaide is also the most convenient capital from which to make a journey to parks in the arid hinterland of NSW, or even to Simpson Desert National Park in the 'corner country' of Queensland.

Climate bears importantly on a choice of destination. Winter on or near the coast is likely to be cold and wet, and summer almost anywhere may be fiercely hot. Winter and spring are the most suitable seasons for visits to the Flinders Ranges and the far northeast. Parks west of Adelaide are at their best in spring and autumn. Midsummer travelling should be limited to the coastal parks of the southeast and Kangaroo Island, which are also pleasant from late spring until well into autumn. South Australia has a general bushfire risk period from November to April. Total fire bans are automatically imposed in some parks for all or most of that time.

Featured parks	Pages
❶ Cleland	48-49
❷ Black Hill	50-51
❸ Flinders Chase	52-53
❹ Seal Bay	54-55
❺ Mt Remarkable	56-57
❻ Flinders Ranges	58-61
❼ Coffin Bay	62
❽ Lincoln	63
❾ Canunda	64-65
❿ Coorong	66

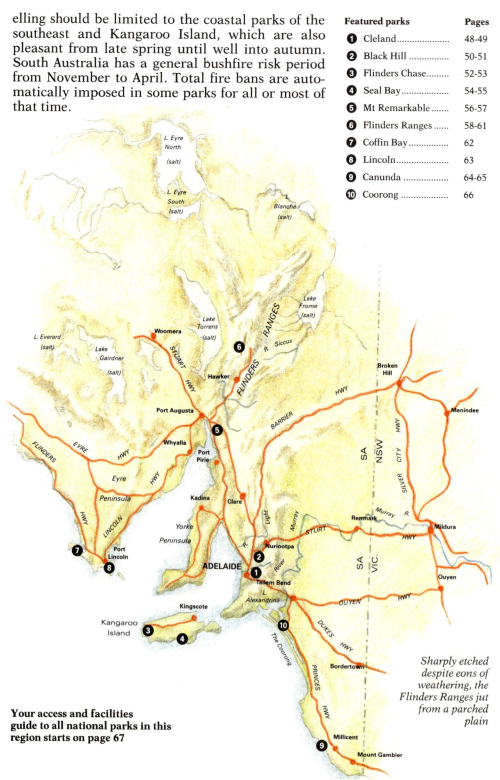

Sharply etched despite eons of weathering, the Flinders Ranges jut from a parched plain

Your access and facilities guide to all national parks in this region starts on page 67

Flowering peas surround a burnt slope where eucalypts are growing back. The blossoms are not native, but relics of Cleland's farming past

CLELAND CONSERVATION PARK

Timbered ridges overlooking Adelaide run west from the summit of Mt Lofty (725 metres) to the rocky gorge of Waterfall Gully. Eucalypt forests and woodlands cover most of Cleland's 890 ha, but king ferns can be found in a few peat bogs. The ferns are relics of a much moister South Australian climate, and are confined now to isolated spots in the Mt Lofty Ranges. There is an excellent network of walking tracks. The pride of Cleland – though largely manmade – is its central native fauna zone. Some exhibits are enclosed, but kangaroos and emus wander freely. Artificial lakes and swamps support waterfowl species rarely seen at such close quarters.

Grass-trees, called yakkas here, border another stand of regenerating eucalypts

Cool creek gullies make for pleasant walking – but alien weeds are common so close to the city

A yakka stands sentinel over introduced butterfly iris

Paterson's curse

Everlasting pea

Eucalypt woodlands crowd to the edges of tilted blocks of sandstone on the windy heights

Black Hill & Morialta Conservation Parks

The 1300 ha of these abutting parks in the Adelaide foothills create a major conservation as well as recreation area close to the city. Grasslands merge into woodlands of river red gum and yellow gum in the northernmost part of Black Hill, but most of the combined area is clothed in eucalypt forests and woodlands dominated by stringybark, on a rough terrain of ridges and steep, rocky gorges. Morialta is noted for its many waterfalls – seen at their best after good rains. Two falls on the Fourth Creek cascade more than 30 metres.

The Black Hill section includes a native plant park and nursery where educational walks can be taken in any season. Other walking tracks cover about 50 km in and between the two main sections; suggested routes take from 45 minutes to 2½ hours. Rock faces in the gorge of Morialta Creek are regarded by climbers as the best within easy reach of Adelaide. But they are dangerous, and call for experience and good equipment. Climbers must be members of approved organisations.

Heavy rain has fed a gushing waterfall in the Morialta section, among steep rock faces that challenge expert climbers

Remarkable Rocks, a richly coloured outcrop on the southwestern shores of Kangaroo Island. Deeper reds are the natural hues of ironstone; vivid orange comes from lichen growth. Some of the most striking coastal scenery is concentrated near Cape du Couedic

Flinders Chase National Park

Picnic grounds are fenced at Rocky River – not to hold people in but to keep animals out. Cape Barren geese and big kangaroos are boldly insistent in their demands for handouts of food, and possums after dark are ready to help themselves. Flinders Chase is South Australia's most important wildlife refuge. The grassy floors of its eucalypt woodlands were never raided by rabbits, and alien predators such as foxes and dingoes did not reach Kangaroo Island. The major native predator is Rosenberg's goanna. Some mammals and many bird species have been introduced from the mainland to ensure their survival. Native birds include the rare western whipbird and the glossy black cockatoo – the latter found nowhere else in the state, although far from rare in eastern Australia.

The park of 73 662 ha occupies a southward-tilting plateau at the western end of the island. It has a rugged coastline of abrupt rocky cliffs and wave-eroded limestone and ironstone formations. Beaches are seldom safe for swimming. Three major rivers dissect the plateau; they flow year-round and their ravines support dense forests. Vehicle tracks radiate from the park headquarters at Rocky River, giving access to some parts of the coast. Marked walking trails, taking 1-3 hours return, reach secluded rivermouths and coves.

Melaleucas and banksias form dense coastal scrubs. Farther inland the park has mallee and stringybark woodlands, and forests dominated by sugar gum

Nobby Island juts from Vivonne Bay, to the west of Seal Bay. Erosion by powerful waves has carved it from the main landmass. Sea lions breed among rocks in the foreground, where visitors are forbidden to walk

Seal Bay Conservation Park

Zierra, a relative of boronia

Sea lions retreat in hundreds from the waterline at Seal Bay on colder days, to shelter in the sandhills. Beyond a mild gaze, they show no concern at the approach of visitors. But these huge marine mammals are not tame – an attempt to touch them will risk a savage bite. The Kangaroo Island colony at Seal Bay accounts for a tenth of the total population of Australian sea lions, and nowhere else are they so easily and reliably seen. They breed in a cycle of about 18 months, after bulls weighing up to 300 kg have fought on the beach for control of harems of cows. Pups are born and nursed in rocky coves at each end of the beach – off-limits to the public.

Bales Beach, to the east, has no restrictions on walking. The water is not suitable for swimming as white pointer sharks frequent this coast. Fishing is forbidden, to protect the sea lions' food stocks. Heaths and mallee woodlands back the eroded limestone cliffs of the 700 ha park and provide a habitat for small and large marsupials.

White-bellied sea-eagles hunt in flight or from perches

Black-eyed Susan

Guinea flower

A sea lion cow is ready to defend her unweaned pup

MOUNT REMARKABLE NATIONAL PARK

Sloping ridges enclose a fertile basin (left) where sheep grazed until the 1960s. Mambray and Alligator Creeks flow quietly through deep gorges (below and right) cut into the sandstone heights. The fancifully named Alligator Creek used to be called Ally's Creek, probably after an Aboriginal stockman

Deep gorges, tree-lined and cool, dissect tilted outcrops of red-brown quartzite sandstone forming the southern Flinders Ranges. Mambray and Alligator Creeks share an oval basin rimmed with sharp ridges – a foretaste of what is seen to the north at Wilpena Pound. Mt Remarkable itself occupies a separate section of the 8649 ha park and is the least visited. But at 995 metres it caps a range that is chiefly responsible for reasonably reliable rains in this district, in contrast to the baked lowlands to the west and south along Spencer Gulf.

River red gums and white cypress pines dot the valleys of the basin, among grasslands where wildflowers bloom brilliantly in early spring. Ridges are wooded with tall sugar gums, distinguished by their piebald grey-and-salmon trunks, and blue gums. Marsupials are abundant along with more than 100 bird species and many reptiles, including the big lace monitor.

Pultenaea

Finger flower

56 ADELAIDE REGION

Flinders Ranges National Park

Saw-toothed ridges slope gently up from the oval green bowl of Wilpena Pound, then fall 1000 metres to an arid outer plain. Walkers reaching the rim look beyond to more tilted ridges. They see the bones of a system of great domed mountains, first pushed up more than 500 million years ago and again about 60 million years ago, of which only stubs of the toughest strata remain. Once the dome of a mountain fold, the Pound has eroded to its quartzite walls and a basin that conforms to the dip of the ancient strata of the Cambrian period.

Higher walls of the ranges catch enough rain to water gorges and valleys for at least part of each year. A wedge of fertility is thrust into the heart of parched Central Australia. Handsome river red gums line the watercourses, and woodlands of cypress pine are widespread. But to botanical purists the very fertility of the Flinders has been their undoing. It meant that every possible area was grazed – in some parts as recently as 1970. Sheep removed most of a natural cover of saltbush. Plants flowering gaily in spring are mostly introduced weeds. Trampling by cattle has changed the character of soils. Rabbits, foxes, dingoes, cats and goats run wild.

None of this detracts from the majesty of the ancient landforms. Wilpena Pound is the most extraordinary feature of the 80 578 ha park, but many of the gorges to the north are its match in scenic attraction, especially when their rivers are running. Red kangaroos abound in open, grassy areas while euros (mountain kangaroos) and rare yellow-footed rock wallabies inhabit the slopes. Reptile species include dangerous king brown, collared brown, black, tiger and death adder snakes, along with 60 kinds of lizards. Their predators, wedge-tailed eagles and nankeen kestrels, wheel overhead.

Many different marked walks, varying in difficulty and taking from an hour to a day, are available in Wilpena Pound or the northern gorges. Longer walks should be attempted only with experience and in suitable weather, after discussion with a ranger.

Left: Remnants of ancient quartzite sandstone ringing Wilpena Pound slope out to a sharp edge, then drop vertically. Below: Seen from across the Pound, the northern rim is surmounted by St Mary Peak (1170 metres), highest point in the ranges

Flash-flooding has stripped away precious soil, exposing the roots of a river red gum

Flinders Ranges National Park

Solanum – potentially poisonous

Tussock grasses dot a high rock outcrop at Bunyeroo Valley, providing ideal habitats for reptiles and birds of prey

Mallee eucalypts indicate drier and less fertile soils. White cypress pine is common on better ground

Coffin Bay National Park

At the heel of Eyre Peninsula a T-shaped platform of limestone and granite juts defiantly into the heavy westerly swells of the great Australian Bight. Coffin Bay Peninsula gives visitors a choice between boisterous surf and gentle, landlocked waters. Swimming and diving are safe at several sandy beaches on either side of the isthmus. Fishing is popular from the shore and from boats, which can be launched at Coffin Bay township or at Point Avoid, where tuna and abalone boats shelter. Coastline features of the 30 380 ha park include striking limestone cliffs, shelving outcrops of smooth granite, active dunefields and scrub-covered dune ridges. Woodlands and richly flowering heathlands surround the quiet inner bays of Port Douglas.

The low granite mass of Golden Island, off Point Avoid, resists the constant pounding of Bight seas. But soft formations of limestone and siltstone on the shore (left) are eroding quickly

Angular pigface in bloom

62 ADELAIDE REGION

Thistle Island, rising beyond smaller islands off Memory Bay in the south of the park, shelters much of the east coast from heavy seas curving round the peninsula

Lincoln National Park

Pimelea

Templetonia retusa

Seaside pastimes are the popular attractions of Lincoln, which occupies most of Jussieu Peninsula at the southeastern end of Eyre Peninsula. Visitor activity is concentrated on the northern shores, facing across quiet waters to Port Lincoln, and at Taylors Landing on the island-sheltered east coast. These parts have the only roads suitable for conventional vehicles, and the only beaches where safe swimming, fishing and boating are assured. Few travellers see the arresting coastal scenery of the wave-battered south, and fewer still know much of the sandy, scrub-covered interior. Most of the 17 372 ha park has no overland walking trails because it fills the role of a nature reserve. Its merging of semi-arid and coastal vegetation and bird habitats is of high scientific interest. Among birds of the scrub are some at the eastern limit of a range that extends to Western Australia.

ADELAIDE REGION 63

Canunda National Park

'Live' sand dunes, drifting inland under the remorseless pressure of westerly winds off the Southern Ocean, uncover and rebury ancient history at Canunda. Old stone dwellings near the resort town of Southport have disappeared. Still older Aboriginal campsites, with fireplaces and shell dumps, have appeared. Where the shifting sands expose former dunes, now solidified, these become low sea cliffs to take the brunt of the ocean's power.

Waves and winds built all of this park, which forms a narrow sand barrier reaching for 40 km between Cape Buffon and Cape Banks. Trapped behind it are flood-prone lowlands and the shallow fresh waters of Lake Bonney. The strip of 9000 ha, averaging about 2 km in width, is a miniature version of the Coorong.

Dense coastal heaths clothe clifftops and stable dunes; swamp plants fringe the wetlands behind. The park is principally a refuge for seabirds, waterfowl and heathland species including the endangered orange-bellied parrot and the seldom-seen rufous bristlebird. Beaches and cliffs are suitable for fishing, but swimming is extremely dangerous from all the beaches. Walking finds little favour: the dunes make hard going.

Eroded limestone remnants of ancient dunes dot nearshore waters at the northern end of the park, providing roosts and nesting grounds for seabirds

Forlorn stumps remain where trees have been swamped and killed by drifting sand. Heavy mineral particles, sinking as the sediments are churned and sifted, make a dark layer at the base of the dune. Below: Salt-tolerant plants colonise an old, solidified dune ridge exposed by winds

Heaths and scrubs crowd a little freshwater lake perched among dunes. But plants growing too close were killed by flooding

Melaleucas fringing the inland side of the Coorong near Woods Well are bowed by the insistent force of winds off the Southern Ocean. These winds also push up the barrier dunes of Younghusband Peninsula, seen in the background

Pelicans and silver gulls hunt for crustaceans. The book and film Storm Boy, *about an Aboriginal youth's affinity with a pelican, were set in this area*

Coorong National Park

Heavy ocean surf and placid lagoon waters are seldom more than 2 km apart along 60 km of coast reaching south from the Murray River 'mouth'. The flow of the depleted river is so feeble, in comparison with the inward thrust of waves and marine sands, that it rarely finds an outlet without help from bulldozers. Instead its silted and salted waters spread sluggishly in Lakes Alexandrina and Albert and down the shallow Coorong, creating perfect wetland habitats for waterfowl.

The park of 38 000 ha, including the Coorong waters as well as the dune barrier of Younghusband Peninsula, embraces a game reserve of nearly 9000 ha where eight wild duck species may be hunted in season. Fishing is popular off the ocean beach and in the Coorong, where conditions are ideal for small boats. A short nature trail near the park headquarters car park, south of Salt Creek, explains the changes in vegetation and in sand dune formation that visitors find in the park.

PARKS OF THE ADELAIDE REGION

FACILITIES

 Cabins
 Caravan park
 Equipped picnic area
 Bush camping allowed
 Lavatory building
 Established campsite
Campsite but no car access

Note: Popular parks without campsites usually have public camping grounds nearby. If in doubt, call enquiries number.

PARK RATINGS No interest ✗ Some interest ✓ Major interest ✓✓ Outstanding ✓✓✓

Belair Recreation Park
13 km S. Central weather district. Car access off Upper Sturt Road, Glenalta. Open 9 am till sunset.
Residential development thins around Belair as Adelaide's suburbs begin to climb into increasingly rugged terrain of the Mt Lofty Ranges. Gentle slopes of the 800 ha park's western section are a major recreation reserve for the city, with sports fields, a golf course, adventure playground, tennis courts and a kiosk. River red gums and peppermint box dominate the remnants of natural vegetation, while extensive stands of mature exotic trees ornament avenues and picnic grounds. Governors of South Australia favoured the area as a summer refuge in the mid-1800s. Their residence has been restored and is now open as a museum.
Deep valleys dissect the park's less disturbed eastern section. Stringybark forests interspersed with pink, blue and manna gum provide a natural environment where walkers see spring wildflowers at their best.
BEST TIME: Spring.
ENQUIRIES: (08) 278 5477.
ADDRESS: Box 2, Belair 5052.

Scenic enjoyment ✓
Day activities ✓✓✓
Family camping ✓✓
Hard bushwalking ✗

Black Hill and Morialta Conservation Parks
12 km NE. Central weather district. Car access off Morialta Road, Rostrevor, and Gorge Road, Athelstone. Closed to cars at sunset.
DESCRIPTION: Page 50.
BEST TIME: Spring, autumn.
ENQUIRIES: (08) 336 3966.
ADDRESS: 115 Maryvale Road, Athelstone 5076.

Scenic enjoyment ✓✓
Day activities ✓✓
Family camping ✗
Hard bushwalking ✓✓✓

Canunda National Park
400 km SE, 26 km W of Millicent. Southeast weather district. Car access off Princes Highway via Southend. Limited park roads for conventional vehicles; full length for 4WD.
DESCRIPTION: Page 65.
NOTES: Permit required for camping. Carry drinking water.
WARNING: Swimming dangerous.
BEST TIME: Spring to autumn.
ENQUIRIES: (087) 35 6053.
ADDRESS: C/o P.O., Southend 5280.

Scenic enjoyment ✓✓
Day activities ✓✓
Family camping ✗
Hard bushwalking ✓

Cleland Conservation Park
9 km SE. Central weather district. Car access off Summit Road, Crafers, and off Waterfall Gully Road, Greenhill. Bus Adelaide-Greenhill Road.
DESCRIPTION: Page 49.
BEST TIME: Spring, autumn.
ENQUIRIES: (08) 339 2581.
ADDRESS: Box 245, Stirling 5152.

Scenic enjoyment ✓✓
Day activities ✓✓✓
Family camping ✗
Hard bushwalking ✓

Coffin Bay National Park
720 km W, 50 km W of Port Lincoln. Western Agricultural weather district. Car access off Flinders Highway 32 km W of Port Lincoln.
DESCRIPTION: Page 62.
NOTES: Permit required for camping. Bush camping restricted to designated sites.
BEST TIME: Spring, autumn.
ENQUIRIES: (086) 85 4047.
ADDRESS: C/o P.O., Coffin Bay 5607.

Scenic enjoyment ✓✓✓
Day activities ✓✓
Family camping ✓
Hard bushwalking ✗

Coorong National Park
210 km SE, 60 km S of Meningie. Southeast weather district. Car access off Princes Highway along inland boundary. Two crossings bridge the Coorong to ocean beaches: 42 Mile Crossing passable year-round; Tea Tree Crossing may be covered by water up to half a metre deep in winter.
DESCRIPTION: Page 66.
NOTES: Access to some islands in Coorong prohibited. Licence required for duck shooting. Permit required for camping.
WARNING: Ocean beaches south of Tea Tree Crossing unsafe for swimming.
BEST TIME: Spring to autumn.
ENQUIRIES: (085) 75 7014.
ADDRESS: Private Bag 43, Meningie 5264.

Scenic enjoyment ✓
Day activities ✓✓
Family camping ✗
Hard bushwalking ✗

Deep Creek Conservation Park
110 km S. Central weather district. Car access off Main South Road at Delamere.
Bushwalkers must be prepared for steep descents as trails through deep valleys of the Mt Lofty Ranges drop to meet the Southern Ocean at the southern end of Fleurieu Peninsula. Sandy pocket beaches just outside the park boundary are reached by walking trails from the major campsites, but most of the park's coastline consists of rocky shores and high cliffs sculpted by relentless ocean swells.
Camping in this 4000 ha park is restricted to undeveloped sites in the tall inland forests of brown stringybark and messmate. The dense scrub understorey contains silver banksia, tea-trees and grass trees. Towards the coast persistent, salt-laden winds stunt the trees: messmates grow in a mallee form and heath plants and pink gum predominate.
NOTES: Permit required for camping. No water supplies in park. Fire ban December-March.
BEST TIME: Spring, autumn.
ENQUIRIES: (085) 59 2263.
ADDRESS: C/o P.O., Delamere 5204.

Scenic enjoyment ✓✓✓
Day activities ✓
Family camping ✗
Hard bushwalking ✓✓

Flinders Chase National Park
210 km SW, 100 km W of Kingscote, Kangaroo Island. Central weather district. Car access off Playford Highway via West End Highway. Car ferry and flights Adelaide-Kangaroo Island; bus Kingscote-Flinders Chase.
DESCRIPTION: Page 53.
NOTES: Permit required for camping; fee charged. Bush camping restricted to designated sites. Fire ban November-March.
WARNINGS: Swimming unsafe. Waves dangerous to walkers at Remarkable Rocks.
BEST TIME: Spring to autumn.
ENQUIRIES: (0848) 37 235.
ADDRESS: Private Bag 246, Rocky River, Kangaroo Island 5223.

Scenic enjoyment ✓✓✓
Day activities ✓✓✓
Family camping ✓✓✓
Hard bushwalking ✓✓

Flinders Ranges National Park
470 km N, 55 km N of Hawker. Northern Agricultural weather district. Hawker-Blinman road crosses park; sealed to Wilpena.
DESCRIPTION: Page 59.
NOTES: Permit required for camping; fee charged. Fire ban November-March. Boil all creek water before drinking.
BEST TIME: Autumn to spring.
ENQUIRIES: Oraparinna section (086) 48 0017; Wilpena section (086) 48 0048.
ADDRESS: Private Bag 22, Hawker 5434.

Scenic enjoyment ✓✓✓
Day activities ✓✓
Family camping ✓✓✓
Hard bushwalking ✓✓✓

Gammon Ranges National Park
680 km N, 265 km N of Hawker. Northeast Pastoral weather district. Car access via Hawker and Copley to Balcanoona.
From the grounds of a former sheep station homestead bushwalkers cross grasslands and pounds dotted with eucalypts, blue-grey mulga and casuarinas to reach rugged cliffs and gorges in the Gammon Ranges. From a distance there seems little relief from the 100 000 ha park's horizon of arid, rocky slopes sparsely dotted with yakkas, cypress pine and hummock grasses. Higher rainfalls on the crest of the main range, however, support dense scrubland dominated by mallee, melaleucas and acacias. In the gullies and gorges semi-permanent creeks foster stands of river red gum and attract a diverse bird population. Parrots move along the tree-lined creeks in big flocks. The gorges also provide an important habitat for yellow-footed rock wallaby colonies, which had to compete for food with feral goats until a control programme in the early 1980s drastically reduced the goats' numbers.
NOTES: Fee charged for camping. Carry drinking water.
BEST TIME: April-October.
ENQUIRIES: (086) 42 3800.
ADDRESS: SANPWS district office, Balcanoona via Copley 5732.

Scenic enjoyment ✓✓
Day activities ✓
Family camping ✗
Hard bushwalking ✓✓✓

Innes National Park
300 km W, 145 km S of Ardrossan. Central weather district. Car access off Highway 1 at Port Wakefield via Ardrossan, Minlaton and Warooka.
A repetitive musical song coming from the dense heath and mallee scrub at the tip of Yorke Peninsula alerted ornithologists in 1965 to the presence of the rare western whipbird. Establishment of a 9000 ha park was principally to preserve the bird's habitat, but it also secured a natural environment around the rugged, cliff-lined coast and its string of popular beaches.
Mallee woodland covers most of the park, enclosing grassy patches and scattered stands of casuarinas and cypress pine. Along the northern shores ridges of stabilised dunes are interrupted by huge sand blowouts drifting inland towards salt marshes and an open growth of tea-tree and cutting grass around a chain of salt lakes. Stunted heath clings to the slopes and headlands exposed to powerful winds blowing off the Southern Ocean.
Surfaced roads ring the park, linking clifftop lookouts, launching ramps, campsites and sheltered bays favoured by anglers and swimmers.
NOTES: Fee charged for camping. Carry drinking water.
WARNING: Clifftops are eroded and may crumble underfoot.
BEST TIME: Spring to autumn.
ENQUIRIES: 011 ask for Stenhouse Bay 12.
ADDRESS: P.O., Stenhouse Bay 5577.

Scenic enjoyment ✓✓✓
Day activities ✓✓✓
Family camping ✓✓✓
Hard bushwalking ✓

PARKS OF THE ADELAIDE REGION

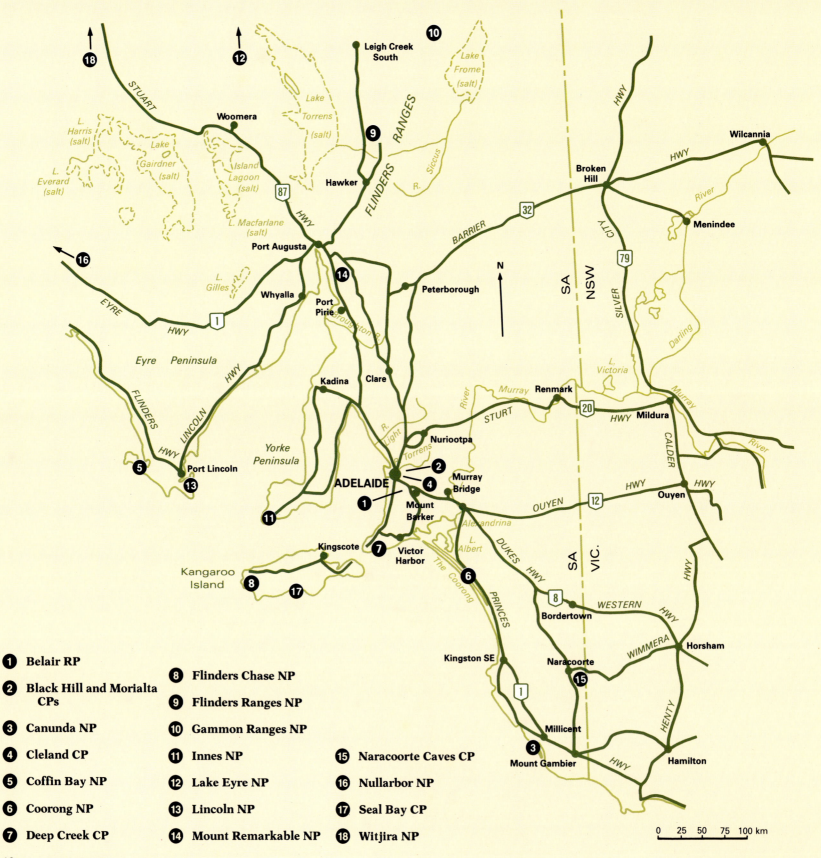

1. Belair RP
2. Black Hill and Morialta CPs
3. Canunda NP
4. Cleland CP
5. Coffin Bay NP
6. Coorong NP
7. Deep Creek CP
8. Flinders Chase NP
9. Flinders Ranges NP
10. Gammon Ranges NP
11. Innes NP
12. Lake Eyre NP
13. Lincoln NP
14. Mount Remarkable NP
15. Naracoorte Caves CP
16. Nullarbor NP
17. Seal Bay CP
18. Witjira NP

PARKS OF THE ADELAIDE REGION

Lake Eyre National Park
900 km N, 100 km NW of Marree. Northeast Pastoral weather district. 4 WD access only.

This vast new park of 1.228 million ha was declared in 1986. The legendary 'inland sea' is both a great salina (dry salt lake) and a great playa lake (one that is occasionally flooded). As salina, its surface was used for the setting of a world land speed record in 1964; as playa, it fills with fish and waterbirds – gulls, pelicans, cormorants, black swans, pink ducks.

The contrast between its two faces is dramatic, but a visit to the region is only for those with a sense of adventure, a love of space and solitude, and a fascination with the sort of wildlife and plants that exist under Eyre's extreme conditions.

Typical vegetation is samphires, saltbush, bluebush and spinifex. The area is home to many species of dragon lizards, geckos and snakes; to tiny marsupial hunters like the mulgara, kowari and dunnart; it is the territory of the wedge-tailed eagle, falcons and harriers.

NOTE: Camping permit required.
WARNING: Visitors must be fully equipped for outback survival. Carry all water and fuel supplies, spare parts and radio transceiver. There are no facilities.
BEST TIME: Cool weather after outback rains. Dangerous in summer.
ENQUIRIES: (086) 75 2499.
ADDRESS: Box 34, Leigh Creek 5731.

Scenic enjoyment ✓✓
Day activities ✗
Family camping ✗
Hard bushwalking ✗

Lincoln National Park
695 km W, 27 km S of Port Lincoln. Western Agricultural weather district. Car access off sealed road 14 km S of Port Lincoln. Internal roads unsealed.
DESCRIPTION: Page 63.
NOTES: No water supplies in park. Permit required for camping.
WARNING: Parts of coastline unsafe for swimming.
BEST TIME: Spring.
ENQUIRIES: (086) 82 3936.
ADDRESS: 90 Tasman Terrace, Port Lincoln 5606.

Scenic enjoyment ✓✓
Day activities ✓✓✓
Family camping ✓✓
Hard bushwalking ✓

Mount Remarkable National Park
270 km N, 50 km N of Port Pirie. Northern Agricultural weather district. Car access to Alligator Gorge off Main North Road at Wilmington; to Mambray Creek off Highway 1, 45 km N of Port Pirie.
DESCRIPTION: Page 56.
NOTES: Permit required for camping: fee charged; bookings recommended for long weekends. Bush camping restricted to designated sites (elsewhere with permission of ranger). No bush camping during total fire ban November-April. Carry drinking water on walks.
BEST TIME: Autumn to spring.
ENQUIRIES: Mambray Creek section (086) 34 7068; Alligator Gorge section (086) 67 5181.
ADDRESS: Private Bag 7, Port Germein 5495.

Scenic enjoyment ✓✓✓
Day activities ✓✓
Family camping ✓✓✓
Hard bushwalking ✓✓✓

Naracoorte Caves Conservation Park
355 km SE, 14 km S of Naracoorte. Southeast weather district. Car access off Naracoorte-Penola road 9 km S of Naracoorte.

Beneath the limestone rock of Cave Range, delicate calcite structures decorate the ceilings and floors of about 60 caves. Three caves with electric light are open daily for guided tours. As well as conical stalactites and stalagmites, waters slowly dripping into the caves have left calcite deposits in thick columns, long hollow tubes and in thin sheets called shawls. Erratic capillary action has formed striking, star-shaped helictites.

Excavations in part of Victoria Cave have uncovered skeletons of many extinct species, including several types of giant marsupial which roamed the region before the cave mouths were blocked by sand some 10 000 years ago. A display has been set up in the cave so that specimens and excavation can be seen together.

Above ground the caves section of this 300 ha park is clothed in forests of brown stringybark and blackwood with an understorey of tea-tree, banksias and wattle. River red gums grow profusely along the banks of Mosquito Creek in the southern part of the park, but the area is regularly inundated in winter and has little attraction for bushwalkers.

NOTES: Permit required for camping; fee charged. Fee charged for entry to caves; tours 9.30-16.00 daily.
VISITOR CENTRE: At park headquarters.
BEST TIME: Year-round.
ENQUIRIES: (087) 62 2340.
ADDRESS: Box 134, Naracoorte 5271.

Scenic enjoyment ✓✓✓
Day activities ✓✓
Family camping ✓✓
Hard bushwalking ✗

Nullarbor National Park
1100 km W, 300 km W of Ceduna. Western Agricultural weather district. Eyre Highway crosses park; rough tracks branch off to coastal cliffs.

Few travellers speeding to distant destinations along the Eyre Highway expect great scenic enjoyment from the vast plain of the Nullarbor. Those who are attracted by signs indicating coastal lookouts, however, are rewarded by stunning views of sheer, high cliffs along the Great Australian Bight. Mallee scrub is patchily distributed in the 230 000 ha park's coastal region, but elsewhere low rainfalls support only a low ground cover of bluebush and saltbush. Grasses and wildflowers appear ephemerally after rains at any time of year, but most frequently in winter.

Subsurface erosion through the plain's level strata of marine limestone has created a number of cave systems. In the absence of trees and heavy vegetation many birds and mammals rely on the caves' shelter to nest and rear their young. Most species, including an important population of hairy-nosed wombats, are nocturnal, emerging in the evening when temperature and humidity are at levels which help contain the loss of body moisture by evaporation.

WARNING: Crumbling cliff edges and strong winds are dangerous along the coast.
BEST TIME: Autumn to spring.
ENQUIRIES: (086) 76 1098.
ADDRESS: SANPWS district office, C/o P.O., Streaky Bay 5680.

Scenic enjoyment ✓✓
Day activities ✓
Family camping ✗
Hard bushwalking ✗

Seal Bay Conservation Park
170 km SW, 60 km SW of Kingscote, Kangaroo Island. Central weather district. See Flinders Chase for island access. Car access off South Coast Road.
DESCRIPTION: Page 55.
NOTE: Fishing prohibited – nearshore waters are a marine reserve.
BEST TIME: Spring to autumn.
ENQUIRIES: (0848) 22 381.
ADDRESS: Box 39, Kingscote 5223.

Scenic enjoyment ✓✓
Day activities ✓✓
Family camping ✗
Hard bushwalking ✗

Witjira National Park
1400 km NNW, 200 km NE of Oodnadatta. Northeast Pastoral weather district. 4 WD access only.

Declared in 1986, the 779 500 ha park extends from the western stony tablelands east to the sand dunes of the Simpson Desert; and from north of Macumba to the flood plains of the Finke River. It protects a unique complex of mound springs.

These are like oases in the desert; permanent sources of water in a land where rainfall is scarce and summer temperatures extreme. The springs are natural outlets for waters from the Great Artesian Basin. As the water evaporates, the minerals it held crystallise and are left behind as solids. Over time they have combined with the ancient sand and clay to form mounds around the spring outlets.

The springs are home to rare fish and amphibia. Because there is permanent water the area has a large and varied bird population.

Traditionally this is the land of the Lower Southern Aranda people. The springs, floodplains and sand dunes are all part of their mythology. Each spring has connection with different ancestors. There are a number of major ritual centres around the Finke.

NOTE: Camping permit required.
WARNING: Visitors must be fully equipped for outback survival. Carry all water and fuel supplies, spare parts and radio transceiver. There are no facilities.
BEST TIME: Cool weather after outback rains. Dangerous in summer.
ENQUIRIES: (086) 75 2499.
ADDRESS: Box 34, Leigh Creek 5731.

Scenic enjoyment ✓✓
Day activities ✗
Family camping ✗
Hard bushwalking ✗

Bearded dragon *Amphibolorus vitticeps* – creature of the inland

Tammar wallaby – lives in coastal scrub or mallee thicket, feeds at night

Fat-tailed dunnart – superb adapter which lives anywhere from the coast to Lake Eyre

Short-beaked echidna – in arid areas active only at night

South Australian wildlife

In spite of the flatness, aridity, high temperatures and sparse vegetation of much of the state it is home territory to an abundance of wildlife. Creatures have adapted to a life with little fresh water and little shelter; most forage at night and shelter in scrub or among rocks during the day. Yellow-footed rock wallabies live where there is apparently no water source; the tammar wallaby is able to drink seawater; birds and various other species do not breed in times of severe drought.

Yellow-footed rock wallaby – inhabitant of dry country it is prey of the wedge-tailed eagle

Wedge-tailed eagle nest – in drought years the birds may not breed

Western grey kangaroos – unlike the eastern grey do not carry a dormant embryo in the uterus while a joey is in the pouch

Birdlife

Peregrine falcon – uses the abandoned nests of other birds

Rock parrot – lives in coastal shrubland and on the islands

Red-rumped parrot – ground-feeding seed-eater

Little penguin – only penguin to breed in Australia

Little corellas – strip the roost tree of all leaves

Pink cockatoo – feeds in branches or on ground on seeds, nuts, fruits and roots

Straw-necked ibis – breeding colonies may contain 200 000 birds

Osprey – young ospreys learn to fish within a week of leaving the nest

73

Visitor activities in the national parks of South Australia

Abseiling (with permits)
Black Hill, Flinders Ranges.

Bird watching
Canunda, Coorong, Deep Creek, Flinders Chase, Flinders Ranges, Gammon Ranges, Innes, Lincoln, Mount Remarkable.

Bush camping
Canunda, Coffin Bay, Coorong, Deep Creek, Flinders Ranges, Gammon Ranges, Innes, Lake Eyre, Lincoln, Mount Remarkable, Nullarbor, Witjira.

Bush walking, including day walks
Black Hill, Cleland, Flinders Chase, Flinders Ranges, major feature at Deep Creek, Gammon Ranges, Mount Remarkable.

Camping
Flinders Chase, Flinders Ranges, Mount Remarkable, Naracoorte.

Canoeing/boating
Coffin Bay, Coorong.

Car touring
Flinders Ranges, Nullarbor. Limited touring in Flinders Chase, Gammon Ranges, Innes, Coorong. With well equipped 4WD at Lake Eyre, Witjira.

Caving (experienced people, with permit)
Naracoorte (a special feature), Nullarbor.

Cave tours
Naracoorte (major attraction).

Cycling
Belair (limited).

Fishing, beach/ocean
Canunda, Coffin Bay, Coorong, Innes (major feature), Lincoln.

Geological studies
Flinders Ranges, Gammon Ranges, Mount Remarkable.

Historical studies
Belair (limited), Flinders Ranges, Gammon Ranges, Innes.

Horse riding (on specified tracks)
Belair, Flinders Ranges.

Photography
Coffin Bay, Coorong, Deep Creek, Flinders Chase, Flinders Ranges, Gammon Ranges, Innes, Lincoln, Mount Remarkable.

Picnicking
Belair, Black Hill, Cleland.

Orienteering (organised groups)
Belair.

Rock climbing (with permits)
Black Hill, Flinders Ranges.

Scuba diving
Innes.

Snorkelling
Innes.

Surfing
Innes (major feature).

Survival skills/journey testing
Lake Eyre, Witjira.

Swimming
Coffin Bay, Coorong, Innes, Lincoln.

Tennis
Belair.

Walking along coastal tracks and beaches
Canunda, Coffin Bay, Flinders Chase, Innes, Lincoln, Seal Bay.

Wildflower studies
Black Hill, Deep Creek, Flinders Chase, Flinders Ranges (spring and after rain).

Wind surfing
Coffin Bay (limited), Coorong.

Yachting
Coffin Bay, Coorong (small yachts; not for beginners), Lincoln.

Wildlife observation
Cleland, Flinders Chase, Seal Bay – special feature of these three parks.

Birdwatchers at Innes National Park, home of the rare western whipbird

South Australian parks provide bush walking for the fit and less demanding walks for those who merely want to wander and enjoy nature

Rock climbing in Morialta Gorge, where the faces are as testing as any in the country

Surfing off Pondalowie Bay at Innes National Park

> **CAMPING**
> **Bush camping** — away from it all, no facilities other than those you create.
> **Camping** — a pit toilet and a tap but no other facilities.
> **Family camping** — established camping ground with showers, toilets, barbecue areas and where you can probably take a caravan, but check beforehand.

The Coorong is a breeding ground for waterbirds and its ocean beach a haunt for fishermen

Dramatic view of the coast through Admiral's Arch in Flinders Chase, at the western end of Kangaroo Island

The native fauna centre at Cleland Conservation Park draws visitors like a magnet. There they may have close-ups of many native animals and birds, but the most popular display is always the koalas

75

MELBOURNE REGION

Forests hold their ground in a crowded corner

VICTORIA is the most densely populated Australian state, and the most intensively farmed. In spite of that nearly a third of its natural bushland remains. Most is mountainous: the Great Dividing Range marches across the state, its outlying ridges pushing to the Bass Strait coast. No other mainland region is so dominated by high country.

National parks in the northeast preserve the lofty plains of the Victorian Alps, snow-covered in winter, but grassy and sprinkled with wildflowers at other times. Parks in the east include wooded upland wildernesses at Croajingolong and Snowy River, temperate rainforests and subtropical remnants at Tarra Valley and Bulga, and an unsurpassed variety of plant communities around the granite peaks of Wilsons Promontory. Ranges in the west are backdrops for remarkable coastal scenery at Otway and Port Campbell. And spacious areas are reserved in highlands fringing Melbourne itself.

With the dedication in 1984 of Grampians National Park, Victoria attained an admirable mark in conservation: more than 5 per cent of its territory is protected in national parks or other professionally managed reserves. In hectares alone the target was not difficult – more than enough mountain terrain lay unused. Finding a representative range of other habitats was harder, but the will was found after a political storm in the late 1960s.

The row centred on obscure sandplains in the remote northwest. Even now they are little visited. A scheme for agricultural expansion threatened one of the last habitats of the malleefowl. The volume of public outcry – and a staggering by-election result – shook the state government. It abandoned the farming plan and proclaimed a vast extension of Little Desert National Park. More significantly, it conceded that piecemeal ways of resolving conflicts over crown land use were not good enough.

A Land Conservation Council was set up in 1970 to plan for the preservation of ecologically important or scenically valuable areas and to meet future needs for public leisure and recreation. Its recommendations, accepted with very little demur by succeeding governments, have led to a dramatic increase in the extent and variety of parks on public land. Completion of the council's programme, to include a few types of natural habitats still missing from the state's array of parks and reserves, calls for the costly resumption of private lands. Shortage of funds is a stumbling block. But Victoria's achievements already are the envy of other states, and of many countries overseas.

Featured parks	Pages	Featured parks	Pages
❶ Brisbane Ranges	78-79	❾ Croajingolong	96-97
❷ Otway	80	❿ Mt Buffalo	98-99
❸ Kinglake	81-83	⓫ Bogong	100-101
❹ Organ Pipes	84	⓬ Port Campbell	102-103
❺ Cape Schanck	85	⓭ Lower Glenelg	104
❻ Wilsons Promontory	86-91	⓮ Mt Eccles	105
❼ Tarra-Bulga	92-94	⓯ Grampians	106-109
❽ Hattah-Kulkyne	95		

Your access and facilities guide to all national parks in this region starts on page 110

Proud achievements in park acquisition are crowned in the Grampians

Grassy glades among forests on the moister slopes may owe their origins to a gold boom at nearby Steiglitz in the 1860s. Many trees were felled to make mine props

Koalas are commonly seen – their natural numbers have been boosted by introductions from Phillip and French Islands in Western Port Bay, east of Melbourne. Kangaroos, wallabies, possums and echidnas also live in the park, with about 150 species of birds

Steiglitz grevillea

Everlastings bloom on a rocky slope of Anakie Gorge, where a river now represented by Stony Creek cut through the ancient slates and shales of the escarpment

Southern grass trees – members of the lily family – thrive on sandy soils. Often they delay putting up their sweet-scented flowering spikes until a bushfire has singed them

Brisbane Ranges National Park

Victoria's richest displays of spring wildflowers are seen here, little more than an hour's drive from Melbourne. The park's 420 native plant species include the unique Brisbane Ranges or steiglitz grevillea and many others that are rare, or cut off from their normal habitats. The unusual geology of the ranges seems to have preserved relics of an age when plants were differently distributed.

A steep scarp forms the eastern edge of the 7500 ha park. It marks the Rowsley Fault, along which the lands of the Port Phillip basin subsided about 1 million years ago. Deep, rocky gullies such as Anakie Gorge now cut into the scarp. To the west the park consists of a gently undulating plateau where eucalypt woodlands have a dense understorey of heaths. Low forests occur on some shale-derived soils.

Bush peas form a dense mat in spring

Curving spurs of the Otway Range reach the westernmost shores of Bass Strait, giving shelter to the Parker River and allowing the sediments it carries to form a delta

Waves and spray working on sandstone of varying hardness produce intriguing shapes on a shore platform

Otway National Park

Broad platforms of wave-worn sandstone skirt cliffs along the Bass Strait shore east of Cape Otway. They make a fascinating pathway for walkers beginning a journey round the cape and along uninhabited Southern Ocean beaches reaching towards Port Campbell. This is a coast of bitter gales and heavy seas, but given fair weather and a fortunate timing of the tides, about 60 km can be traversed, at or near the waterline, in four or five days.

The eastern section of the 12 750 ha park includes an inland wedge taking in the catchments of the Calder, Parker and Elliott Rivers in the Otway Range. A high rainfall supports towering forests of mountain ash on protected slopes, and gullies of myrtle beech rainforest with thick undergrowths of mosses and tree ferns. Short forest walks can be taken from Maits Rest on the Great Ocean Road. Wallabies and possums are commonly seen. Bower birds and king parrots are among many species of birds in the park.

Kinglake National Park

Cool, fern-filled gullies contrast agreeably with slopes of dry eucalypt forest running towards Melbourne from the Kinglake ridge, where the Great Dividing Range curves closest to the city. North-south spurs 400-500 metres high are separated by the valleys of streams that drop sharply – cascading after good rains – to the lowlands before joining the Yarra River. Each of the three sections of the 11 400 ha park, which has been pieced together from land long since deserted by farmers, miners and timber getters, offers at least half a dozen different walks that sample the varying scenery. Some have steep pinches, but they command excellent views over the foothills and plains surrounding Melbourne. Lyrebirds are numerous, though not often seen; the males can be heard practising their mimicry in winter.

More than 30 species of ferns have been identified in the steep, damp gullies of Kinglake

Goodenia ovata can grow up to 2 metres in mountain forests

Musk daisies thrive in gullies, often emerging over tree ferns

Double-tails orchid

Kinglake National Park

Left: Wombelano Falls plunges from densely forested heights in the park's northern section – the most challenging area for bushwalkers

Tall eucalypts crowd a well-watered hillside – but the bracken floor indicates a recent fire

Organ Pipes National Park

Plants grow readily in the rich Keilor Plains soils on and around the Organ Pipes, but weeds are a problem – the area was cleared and used for grazing for 130 years

Towering columns of basalt were formed from a million-year-old lava flow that filled a river valley, then split as it cooled and shrank. A later earth movement tilted the structure, and now the valley wall that concealed it has been stripped away by the action of Jacksons Creek. Close views are gained on an easy walk of about 800 metres. Other features of the 85 ha park seen on longer walks include Rosette Rock, where columns radiate like the spokes of a wheel, and the Tessellated Pavement, where the creek has worn other columns down to ground level and left what look like hexagonal tiles.

Cape Schanck Coastal Park

Wave erosion on a southern tongue of Cape Schanck eats at soft rock behind a more resistant pillar. Eventually it will stand alone as a nearshore stack. Right: Wind-driven spray and sand etch flowing contours in layered sandstone. But its capping of limestone, from an ancient dune, wears at a far slower rate

Clifftops and dunes backing a string of noted surfing beaches are reserved for public recreation along almost all of the Bass Strait side of Mornington Peninsula, from Portsea to beyond the Cape Schanck lighthouse. It is a windswept coast, frequently battered by heavy seas. Woodlands once ran to the cliff edges, but the area was cleared and grazed before 1870. The scrubs that have taken over since are stunted and sparse, and where they are damaged there are serious problems of soil erosion and dune movement. Rock formations provide the natural highlights of the 1095 ha park. Short walks are described in leaflets. Experienced walkers can cover the 28 km length of the park in one or two daily stages – but camping is not permitted.

Mt Bishop is a typical granite tor, formed of upthrust molten material and now exposed by the erosion of softer overlying rock

Tannin from decaying plant matter stains Tidal River, near the main camping area

WILSONS PROMONTORY NATIONAL PARK

Seaweeds swish in gentle currents at Waterloo Bay

'The Prom' is so popular with Victorians that holiday cabins must be balloted for, and a permit system operates to control the numbers taking overnight hikes. Solitude is possible, however, around remote bays and inlets. Six peaks stand above 500 metres. More than 80 km of marked walking tracks crisscross the 49 000 ha park. Most of them lead to sandy beaches in the shelter of striking headland formations.

Plant life is exceptionally varied. Many of the 700 species of flowering plants and ferns are uncommon, or found elsewhere only in Tasmania. Eucalypt forests dominate the high country, and include some tall mountain ash. Protected east-facing slopes have temperate rainforest zones, with myrtle beech in some gullies. Exposed slopes support eucalypt or banksia woodlands. There are also grasslands and extensive swamps. Corner Inlet even has a scattering of stunted mangroves – the southernmost in the world.

Lichen-coated granite boulders defy the elements at Picnic Point. Islands of the Glennie group, visible in the distance, are included in the park along with a dozen others close to 'The Prom'. Left: A flat beach at Whisky Bay makes a take-off runway for terns after a feast of fish and crustaceans. Nearby islands are important breeding grounds for many species of seabirds, including penguins. The promontory is also a resting place for many other birds on their north-south migratory routes

Wilsons Promontory National Park

A chilly midwinter sea, calm in the shelter of Waterloo Bay, laps dazzling sands eroded from granite rich in quartz and feldspar

Mist conceals the peaks of the Wilson Range, rising steeply behind sandy beaches at Tidal River. The river has its outlet in a tightly sheltered corner of Norman Bay, halfway down the western side of the promontory. Boulders on the intertidal fringe (below) are coated with moss

Casuarinas and ferns, including uncommon gleichenia or coral fern (left foreground), crowd a deep, wet gully beside the track to Waterloo Bay

Wilsons Promontory National Park

Granite tors studding the slopes of Mt Boulder (500 metres) orginated more than 300 million years ago as magma thrusting up into sedimentary rock

Tarra-Bulga National Park

Declared in 1986, this park of 1230 ha combines the former Bulga and Tarra Valley National Parks in the eastern Strzelecki Ranges. It has significant stands of cool temperate rainforest and a varied and prolific population of ferns. Highlight of the Bulga section is Fern Gully, where there are more than 30 fern species. Another pleasure, in the Tarra Valley, is the Cyathea Falls, tumbling down a faulted slope of the ranges. Walking tracks in the park cross slopes of mountain ash, myrtle beech and sassafras. Among the abounding birdlife are lyrebirds, olive whistlers and robins.

Filmy ferns

Leaves of myrtle beech

Among Bulga's profusion of ferns are the kangaroo fern (left), an epiphyte that attaches itself to trees, and soft tree ferns (below). Along the scenic track skirting the north side of the park (right), tall eucalypts emerge from a dense understorey of rainforest character

Constant moisture at the Cyathea Falls fosters luxuriant fern growth. Rainfall is high, and sunlight and drying winds rarely penetrate the gully

Hattah-Kulkyne National Park

In contrast to its ending at the Coorong, the Murray River is master upstream of Mildura. At Hattah its periodic flooding has created an oasis of leafy woodlands among the semi-arid grasslands and sand ridges of northwestern Victoria and far western NSW. Floodwaters spill west along Chalka Creek to replenish a system of intermittent wetlands and a dozen lakes, securing the breeding grounds of scores of waterfowl species.

River red gums crowd the lake shores and sometimes grow among black box on higher ground, where extraordinary floods of the past have allowed them to seed. Other trees characteristic of the 40 000 ha park are buloke casuarina, eumong acacia and white cypress pine. Wildflowers, abundant in spring, have replaced some forest stands that were cleared for timber and grazing. A short self-guided nature walk starts near the park entrance and takes no more than 45 minutes.

Gracefully twisting river red gums line the Murray, which forms a winding eastern boundary to the park. These trees thrive on flooding – but here it endangers them because powerful currents erode the bank and expose their roots

Winds eat a path through dunes behind Point Hicks, which is thought to have been the first Australian landfall on James Cook's exploratory voyage in 1770. Sand-binding plants in the foreground are true spinifex – their name is wrongly given to hummock grasses of arid hinterland regions

Sands pushed in by powerful waves make a lagoon of the Thurra River's estuary. Storm surges and spring tides break the barrier periodically, flushing out the waterway. Scrubs and heaths on the dunes make ideal habitats for the rare eastern bristlebird and ground parrot

Croajingolong National Park

Naturalists rank Croajingolong as one of the most interesting parks in Victoria, and among the most significant in Australia. In 86 000 ha it has elements of three widely differing vegetation types: cool-temperate communities like Tasmania's, soft-leafed subtropical plants in common with coastal NSW, and species adapted to fierce drought and fire regimes.

The range of animal life is correspondingly wide. Contrasts in scenery are bold. Steep, forested ridges and gullies – the catchments of dozens of streams – run south from a dissected tableland to an intricate coastline of cliffs, vast dune systems, lakes and tightly enclosed inlets, moulded by the persistent wave power of Bass Strait.

A seaboard of 100 km, from the NSW border to Sydenham Inlet, is of chief interest to holidaymakers. It has Victoria's mildest year-round climate – though a peculiarity of the district is its dry electrical storms in summer. Gale-driven bushfires did extensive damage in 1983, but little is evident round the inlets where visitors concentrate their activities. The park skirts the busy boating and fishing resort at Mallacoota Inlet and extends to quieter spots to the west, reached by unsealed roads.

Dry forests of eucalypts and angophoras cloak Croajingolong's steep inland ridges

Waves working on a cliff base of folded, tilted rock near Mallacoota Inlet are slowly creating an archway. Mallacoota was a reserve as early as 1909, along with Wingan Inlet. Small national parks in these two localities, and Captain James Cook National Park at Point Hicks, were absorbed into Croajingolong in 1979

Mountain gentian, blooming in February

Mountain gums force open a rock cleft that was created by frost

Crystal Brook flows tranquilly towards the Eurobin Falls in summer. But the wear on the boulders tells of a violent torrent when the snows melt each spring

The sheer plateau walls to be found in Mt Buffalo National Park – where many rocky peaks exceed 1500 metres – offer some of the hardest climbs in Australia

MOUNT BUFFALO NATIONAL PARK

Paper daisies

Massive bluffs and towering, near-vertical, granite walls punctuate the extensive Buffalo Plateau, soaring 1000 metres above the Ovens Valley. Granite tors stud the tops which are snow-covered in winter; in the 1930s, Buffalo became Victoria's first skiing playground. At the southern edge, a rocky pyramid reaches 1723 metres. Called the Horn, it puts the finishing touch to the animal silhouette that prompted early explorers to give the plateau its name. Many other peaks in the 31 000 ha park exceed 1500 metres. Buttresses and almost sheer walls – especially at the Gorge, above Eurobin Falls – offer rock climbers some of the most varied and challenging faces in Australia.

Wildflowers deck the alpine grasslands and heaths in summer, among woodlands of snow gum. Eucalypt forests on the lower slopes include candlebark, mountain gum and alpine ash. Walkers can choose from 140 km of tracks. They include nature trails at the Gorge, Dicksons Falls and View Point – all accessible on a brief visit. Canoeing is popular on Lake Catani.

Alpine heaths struggle for survival on the rocky edge of the Bogong plateau

Bogong National Park

Eleven of Victoria's 12 highest summits cluster here, in the state's biggest tract of alpine country. Mt Bogong (1986 metres) stands supreme in the northernmost corner of the 81 200 ha park. Most of it is tablelands, offering cross country skiers unrivalled scope in winter. Falls Creek and Mt Hotham, alpine resorts, are outside the park but practically enclosed by its boundaries.

Flowers blossom brilliantly on grassy upland slopes and bogs in summer, above a belt of snow gum woodlands. Mountain gum and alpine ash dominate lower forests, with black sallee and dense fern understoreys in some gullies. Marsupials and native birds are abundant. Walks of varying difficulty cover most of the park.

Blossoms of the alpine strawflower and hairy cutleaf daisy (far right) ornament the high plains late in summer

Seen from above, columns of basalt look like paving stones. They are made of volcanic lava that shrank and split as it cooled. At the Ruined Castle (right) later earth movements have snapped the columns

Horizontal layers of limestone stand out clearly in Island Arch. Waves and spray have found a weak spot in the middle and are eating out a hole. This formation is just offshore from Loch Ard Gorge, which was named after the most disastrous of six shipwrecks near Port Campbell. Of 54 people aboard the Loch Ard in 1878 only two survived – an 18-year-old cabin boy and a girl passenger of the same age. The boy, Tom Pearce, scaled the gorge to fetch help. Four victims are buried on the clifftop

Port Campbell National Park

Limestone is no match for the wave power of the Southern Ocean. Travellers on the Great Ocean Road, for about 12 km on either side of Port Campbell, see a coastline in rapid retreat. It is carved in an erratic pattern of gorges, archways, blowholes and sheer cliffs where huge slabs, undercut by the tides and weakened above by rain seepage, have collapsed and been pulverised. Seas boil around tougher remnants, isolated as nearshore stacks.

Excellent vantage points are gained by side roads or on foot from marked points on the highway. A self-guided 'discovery walk' taking 1½ hours starts near Port Campbell beach. Smaller beaches are accessible at Loch Ard Gorge, Sherbrooke River and below Gibson Steps. Coastal scrubs and heaths cloak clifftops and gorges in the 1750 ha park. A big seabird population may include penguins, and shearwaters nest on Muttonbird Island.

London Bridge, off the western end of the park towards Peterborough, will eventually collapse and two separate stacks will be left. The Twelve Apostles (some seen at right) are probably remnants of a bigger formation that went through a similar process. The ocean is claiming back what it created some 25 million years ago, when this part of the continental mass lay under water. Marine deposits of shell and skeletal debris built a paving 250 metres thick. When the land rose later, this became a limestone plateau – now all too easily eroded

Lower Glenelg National Park

Nearing the end of its 400 km course from the Grampians, the Glenelg River cuts a deep gorge through the limestone of an ancient sea bed. The gorge and its bordering eucalypt forests are protected for a length of 35 km. In the eastern part of the 27 300 ha park, the Kentbruck Heath is noted for spring wildflowers, including more than 50 species of ground orchids.

Unsealed roads and walking tracks reach a variety of ferny gullies, river and gorge viewing points and a coastal lookout. The river is accessible at many spots; swimming and fishing are popular and small boats are easily launched. Many cave systems have been discovered deep in the limestone. The Princess Margaret Rose Caves, 15 km north of Nelson, are open daily for tours.

Acacias and eucalypts overhang the Glenelg River above its entry to the gorge. The river is a breeding ground for many ocean fish. Anglers make good catches of bass, black bream, mulloway and Australian salmon between October and May. Left: Moleside Creek, a swift-running tributary of the Glenelg, originates in the low hills of the colourful Kentbruck Heath

Lake Surprise, ringed with eucalypt woodlands, seems to be fed by underground springs. Its level falls each summer but returns during the winter to a maximum depth of 13 metres. Swimming and boating are allowed, but boats have to be carried down a steep stairway

Hot gases once poured from this vent in the crater flanks, giving the volcano a safety valve. Later such fissures provided shelter for Aboriginal hunting parties, or roosts for insect-eating bats

MOUNT ECCLES NATIONAL PARK

Manna gum woodlands end abruptly on the stony cliffs rimming Lake Surprise. Tranquil green waters fill a cavity like a giant bathtub, more than 700 metres long and 180 metres wide. Below are the blocked vents of one of Australia's most recent volcanoes, active between 10 000 and 6000 years ago.

Mt Eccles, a rounded cone prominent above the southeastern edge of the craters, is not itself a volcano. It is a heap of debris, windblown from successive eruptions. The slopes – dangerously unstable to walk on – are of scoria, a light rock made from bubbly lava.

Safer walks, taking from 20 minutes to 2 hours, lead around the cliffs and the wooded edges of the lake. Along the route of an old lava flow at the northern end is a cave of basalt, big enough to enter. Solidified drips of lava hang from the ceiling like stalactites. No greater variety of volcanic forms can be so easily seen as in this park 5470 ha in area.

Dry eucalypt forests crowd a tough ridge of sandstone in the Serra Range. Peregrine falcons nest in its crannies

Grampians National Park

Victoria gained its biggest – 167 000 ha – and most imposing national park in 1984. In the former Grampians State Forest, forestry and grazing were already tightly zoned, and much of the area was handed over in a natural state with public amenities such as camping grounds and picnic areas widely provided. Motorists and bushwalkers alike have unrivalled scope to roam among striking landforms and richly diverse vegetation on the westernmost heights of the Great Divide.

Folded sandstones form a series of weathered ranges running north-south for about 100 km. The highest point, Mt William in the east, is 1168 metres and many other summits exceed 800 metres. Most of the ranges have steep scarps on their eastern sides but slope gently to the west. The park surrounds three sizeable reservoirs where boating and fishing are popular, and includes countless creeks and streams. There are numerous walking tracks to all the major scenic features; the Wonderland area, near Halls Gap, is the most fascinating and accessible.

Eucalypts dominate the forests and woodlands, but sightseers are especially attracted to the high heaths and their brilliant floral displays between August and November. Nearly 900 flowering species – including 100 orchids – are found in the park and several are found nowhere else. Over 200 bird species have been recorded. Mammals include the endangered brush-tailed rock wallaby.

The Balconies, near Halls Gap, command sweeping views south

Aboriginal paintings decorate Flat Rock Shelter. Tribes from both north and south shared occupation of the Grampians

Below: Sandstone faces of the Grand Canyon are deeply etched by rain and chemical action

A rich pocket of iron succumbs to water erosion

Eucalypts on dry slopes (left) suffer frequent fire damage, but tree ferns (right) survive as rainforest relics in deep gullies

GRAMPIANS NATIONAL PARK

The Broken Falls, on the McKenzie River, are formed from an intrusion – called a dyke – of porphyritic rock. It is volcanic in origin, and much harder than the usual sandstone of the Grampians

PARKS OF THE MELBOURNE REGION

FACILITIES

 Cabins
 Caravan park
 Equipped picnic area
 Bush camping allowed
 Lavatory building
 Established campsite
Campsite but no car access

Note: Popular parks without campsites usually have public camping grounds nearby. If in doubt, call enquiries number.

PARK RATINGS No interest ✗   Some interest ✓   Major interest ✓✓   Outstanding ✓✓✓

Alfred National Park
470 km E, 18 km E of Cann River. East Gippsland weather district. Princes Highway crosses park.

Bushfires badly damaged much of this rare enclave of Victorian warm-temperate rainforest when they swept through the 2300 ha park in 1983. It will take many years before the complex balance of vegetation in the deep, moist gullies is regained. More than 40 fern species have been identified in the park. They include the rare oval fork fern and prickly tree fern.

Short trails will help visitors avoid dense, leech-infested undergrowth on walks around rainforest pockets. Fire trails lead to a granite ridge which caps the park with the three peaks over 400 metres. The surrounding forest, seen from the highway, is dominated by eucalypts growing over a profusion of wattles.
NOTE: No camping in park.
BEST TIME: Year-round.
ENQUIRIES: (051) 58 6351.
ADDRESS: Park office, Princes Highway, Cann River 3889.

Scenic enjoyment ✓✓
Day activities ✓✓
Family camping ✗
Hard bushwalking ✗

Baw Baw National Park
200 km E, 60 km N of Moe. West Gippsland weather district. Car access off Princes Highway via Thomson Valley Road north of Erica (last 13 km unsealed).

Snow gum woodland and a dense understorey of flowering shrubs grows to the highest ridges and peaks of the Baw Baw Plateau, a mountainous block at the southern end of Victoria's high country. Extensive treeless tracts of sub-alpine bog and peaty swamps form on poorly drained, lower-lying ground where a number of major rivers begin their courses to steep, heavily forested gullies at the edge of the 13 300 ha park.

Short walking trails into the park meet a 20 km section of the Apline Walking Track traversing the plateau from north to south past Mt St Phillack (1566 metres) and Mt Erica (1524 metres). Above 1200 metres snow covers the ground from July to September and many summer hiking tracks become cross-country ski touring routes. The Alpine Village, a downhill skiing centre outside the park and approached via Drouin, can be used as a starting point.
NOTES: Carry snow chains in winter and ensure car radiators contain anti-freeze. Permit required for walking in Mount Whitelaw area. Bush camping not permitted in Mount Whitelaw area. All bush campers should contact park ranger before setting out. Licence required for trout fishing.
WARNING: Severe weather changes occur suddenly. Ski tourers and bush campers must be adequately equipped to cope with emergencies.
BEST TIME: Year-round.
ENQUIRIES: (051) 65 3481.
ADDRESS: Box 63, Rawson 3825.

Scenic enjoyment ✓✓✓
Day activities ✓✓
Family camping ✓✓
Hard bushwalking ✓✓✓

Bogong National Park
375 km, 93 km SE of Myrtleford. Northeast weather district. Car access off Ovens Highway via Mount Beauty to Falls Creek or via Harrietville to Mount Hotham. Coaches to Falls Creek and Mount Hotham in ski season.
DESCRIPTION: Page 100.
NOTES: No camping within 200 metres of public roads or within 30 metres of streams. Overnight walkers should carry tents: huts may be full or difficult to find. Licence required for fishing.
WARNING: Severe weather changes occur suddenly; carry adequate clothing and emergency rations.
BEST TIME: Year-round (summer for flowers).
ENQUIRIES: (057) 57 2693.
ADDRESS: Box 180, Mount Beauty 3699.

Scenic enjoyment ✓✓
Day activities ✓
Family camping ✓✓
Hard bushwalking ✓✓✓

Brisbane Ranges National Park
105 km W. Central weather district. Car access off Western Freeway along Ballan-Geelong road.
DESCRIPTION: Page 79.
NOTES: Bookings required for the small campsite. Bush camping in designated areas only.
BEST TIME: Autumn to spring.
ENQUIRIES: (052) 84 1230.
ADDRESS: C/o P.O., Anakie 3221.

Scenic enjoyment ✓✓
Day activities ✓✓
Family camping ✓
Hard bushwalking ✓

Burrowa-Pine Mountain National Park
420 km NE. Northeast weather district. Car access off Murray Valley Highway to Cudgewa or off Tallangatta-Corryong road. Cudgewa-North Walwa road (dry weather) passes through park.

The isolated dome of Pine Mountain (1062 metres) with its exposed faces of red granite rises steeply from the Murray River plain. Like most areas in the 17 600 ha park, the mountain's summit can only be reached by walkers trekking through trackless bush. But the effort is rewarded with panoramic views to the Snowy Mountains in the north and to the mountainous block around 1300 metre Mt Burrowa in the south.

Broad valleys cleared for farming surround the park which consists of two mountainous blocks linked by an L-shaped corridor. Snow gums grow around Mt Burrowa on peaks where snow may lie for several weeks in winter. Red cypress pines and kurrajong predominate on the dry slopes of Pine Mountain, and the area is noted for a number of rare plants, including the phantom wattle and Pine Mountain grevillea. A short walking track leads from the picnic and camping area at the end of Falls Road (off Cudgewa-North Walwa Road) to the impressive Cudgewa Bluff Falls.
NOTES: Water scarce in summer.
BEST TIME: Autumn and spring.
ENQUIRIES: (060) 77 4284.
ADDRESS: Box 74, Cudgewa 3705.

Scenic enjoyment ✓✓
Day activities ✓✓
Family camping ✓
Hard bushwalking ✓✓

Cape Schanck Coastal Park
90 km S. Central weather district. Car access off Nepean Highway between Rosebud and Portsea. Vehicle entrance fee in summer. Buses Frankston-Portsea.
DESCRIPTION: Page 85.
NOTES: No camping in park. Surf patrols at Gunnamatta Beach and Portsea Back Beach during weekends and holidays in summer.
BEST TIME: Spring to autumn.
ENQUIRIES: (059) 84 1586.
ADDRESS: Box 117, Sorrento 3943.

Scenic enjoyment ✓✓
Day activities ✓✓
Family camping ✗
Hard bushwalking ✓✓

Churchill National Park
32 km SE. Central weather district. Car access off Stud Road, Rowville. Buses along Stud Road daily.

Though less than 200 ha in area, Churchill preserves a fine sample of plant species typical of Dandenong foothills woodland. A small patch of messmate and narrow-leafed peppermint forest grows on high ground along the northern boundary, but most of the fenced-in park is covered by open woodland dominated by swamp gum, manna gum, black wattle and dogwood. These species have been able to recolonise the area after clearing for electricity transmission lines, stone quarrying and the ravages of bushfires.

Many small mammals have survived in the park, but they are mostly nocturnal. Visitors are more likely to see kangaroos, wallabies and wombats reintroduced to the park after the original populations died out. A bend in one of the walking trails is noted for its colony of bellbirds, recognised by the bell-like notes of their song.
NOTE: No camping in park.
BEST TIME: Spring to autumn.
ENQUIRIES: (03) 700 4700.
ADDRESS: C/o P.O., Rowville 3178.

Scenic enjoyment ✓
Day activities ✓✓
Family camping ✗
Hard bushwalking ✗

---

1. Alfred NP
2. Baw Baw NP
3. Bogong NP
4. Brisbane Ranges NP
5. Burrowa-Pine Mountain NP
6. Cape Schanck Coastal Park
7. Churchill NP
8. Cobberas-Tingaringy NP
9. Croajingolong NP
10. Fern Tree Gully NP
11. Fraser NP
12. Grampians NP
13. Hattah-Kulkyne NP
14. Kinglake NP
15. Lind NP
16. Little Desert NP
17. Lower Glenelg NP
18. Mitchell River NP
19. Morwell NP
20. Mount Buffalo NP
21. Mount Eccles NP
22. Mount Richmond NP
23. Organ Pipes NP
24. Otway NP
25. Port Campbell NP
26. Snowy River NP
27. Tarra-Bulga NP
28. The Lakes NP

PARKS OF THE MELBOURNE REGION

- ㉙ Wilsons Promontory NP
- ㉚ Wonnangatta-Moroka NP
- ㉛ Wyperfeld NP

Cobberas-Tingaringy National Park
450 km NE, 80 km N of Buchan. East Gippsland weather district. Car access north of Buchan along roads to Suggan Buggan and Bonang.
  Mountainous terrain cut by fast-flowing, rapids-strewn rivers and the narrow gorges of their tributaries make up much of this 107 000 ha park. A great variety of rock types, and altitudes ranging from 160 metres to 1838 metres at Mt Cobberas, ensure an ever-changing landscape with panoramic views from ridges and mountain peaks. Diverse vegetation includes alpine herbfields and grasslands, slopes of cypress pine and white box in drier areas, sheltered gullies of mountain rainforest and alpine woodlands of snow gum.
  Snow covers the high plains and ridges in winter, providing excellent opportunities for cross-country skiing. In summer hikers take extended bushwalks along fire trails and undeveloped though well-used wilderness routes. Wide sandy beaches along the Snowy River near Mackillop Bridge are suitable for swimming, while rapids upstream, challenge experienced canoeists.
WARNING: Snowy River may rise rapidly, becoming dangerous to swimmers and canoeists.
BEST TIME: Spring to autumn.
ENQUIRIES: (0648) 8 0277.
ADDRESS: Deddick via Bonang 3888.

Scenic enjoyment ✓✓✓
Day activities ✓
Family camping ✓✓
Hard bushwalking ✓✓✓

Croajingolong National Park
500 km E, 20 km S of Cann River. East Gippsland weather district. Car access off Princes Highway between Cann River and Genoa. Train Melbourne-Bairnsdale, bus Bairnsdale-Mallacoota.
DESCRIPTION: Page 97.
NOTES: Bookings and fee required for all four campsites. Licence required for fishing.
BEST TIME: Spring to autumn.
ENQUIRIES: (051) 58 6372.
ADDRESS: As for Alfred.

Scenic enjoyment ✓✓✓
Day activities ✓✓✓
Family camping ✓✓✓
Hard bushwalking ✓✓

Fern Tree Gully National Park
34 km E. Central weather district. Car access off Burwood Highway. Vehicle entrance fee. Trains Melbourne-Upper Ferntree Gully.
  A network of easy walking tracks with abundant picnic facilities and views of Melbourne and Port Phillip Bay makes Fern Tree Gully a major weekend attraction in the Dandenong Ranges. More than 300 000 people visit the 460 ha park each year.
  A thick growth of eucalypts and tree ferns has been re-established along Fern Tree Gully Creek with the help of intensive weed control and fencing. A stepped path follows the creek's course down One Tree Hill (503 metres), which was cleared last century.
  Poorer soils on slopes and ridges away from the main gully support a low eucalypt forest dominated by red stringybarks, long-leafed box and peppermint.
NOTE: Gates close at 8 pm in summer, sunset in other seasons.
BEST TIME: Year-round.
ENQUIRIES: (03) 758 1001.
ADDRESS: Box 21, Upper Ferntree Gully 3156.

Scenic enjoyment ✓✓
Day activities ✓✓✓
Family camping ✗
Hard bushwalking ✗

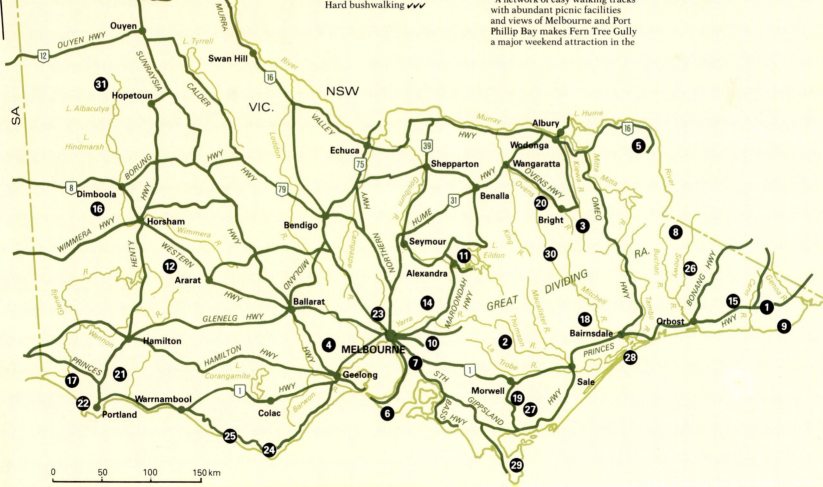

PARKS OF THE MELBOURNE REGION

Fraser National Park
165 km NE, 17 km E of Alexandra. North Central weather district. Car access off Goulburn Valley Highway.

A number of farms disappeared when the valleys of the Goulburn and Delatite Rivers were flooded in the early 1950s to create Lake Eildon to provide extra irrigation for the lower Goulburn Valley. Fraser National Park was established in 1957 on former grazing land on the western shore of Lake Eildon.

Hillsides surrounding the lake have been extensively cleared, both by farmers and by the gold prospectors who came before them. In the absence of grazing, forests of red stringybark, narrow and broad-leafed peppermint, red box and silver wattle are returning.

The 3750 ha park is generously equipped with lakeshore camping and picnic facilities for the convenience of visitors mostly interested in swimming, canoeing and power boating. The regenerating forests can be explored along a web of formed tracks climbing spurs and gullies to commanding ridge-top lookouts.
NOTES: Fee charged for camping. Bookings required during holidays. Licence required for fishing.
BEST TIME: Spring to autumn.
ENQUIRIES: (057) 72 1293.
ADDRESS: Box 153, Alexandra 3714.

Scenic enjoyment ✓✓
Day activities ✓✓✓
Family camping ✓✓✓
Hard bushwalking ✓

Grampians National Park
280 km W, 25 km SW of Stawell. Wimmera weather district. Car access off Western Highway from Stawell, Ararat and Horsham; off Glenelg Highway from Dunkeld.
DESCRIPTION: Page 106.
NOTES: Camping not permitted in water catchment or scientific reference areas and Wonderland section. Booking required for camping at Zumstein; fee charged. Fourteen other areas available – no booking or fee. Licence required for fishing.
WARNINGS: Severe weather changes occur suddenly; bushwalkers should carry adequate warm clothing. Rock slides may occur in broken or steep areas.
BEST TIME: Late winter and spring.
ENQUIRIES: (053) 56 4381 or 82 5011.
ADDRESS: Box 18, Halls Gap 3381.

Scenic enjoyment ✓✓✓
Day activities ✓✓✓
Family camping ✓✓✓
Hard bushwalking ✓✓✓

Hattah-Kulkyne National Park
430 km NW, 39 km N of Ouyen. Mallee weather district. Car access off Murray Valley Highway 4 km E of Hattah.
DESCRIPTION: Page 95.
NOTES: Bush camping restricted to designated sites with permission of ranger. Carry water supplies. NSW licence required for river fishing; Victorian licence for lakes.
VISITOR CENTRE: Park entrance.
BEST TIME: Autumn, spring.
ENQUIRIES: (050) 29 3253.
ADDRESS: RSD Hattah 3501.

Scenic enjoyment ✓✓
Day activities ✓✓✓
Family camping ✓✓✓
Hard bushwalking ✓✓

Kinglake National Park
65 km NE. Central weather district. Car access off Yarra Glen-Yea road and Steels Creek road north of Yarra Glen.
DESCRIPTION: Page 81.
NOTES: Bookings and permit required for camping. Fee charged at Masons Falls picnic area.
BEST TIME: Spring to autumn.
ENQUIRIES: (057) 86 5351.
ADDRESS: National Park Road, Pheasant Creek 3757.

Scenic enjoyment ✓✓✓
Day activities ✓✓✓
Family camping ✓✓
Hard bushwalking ✓✓

Lind National Park
425 km E. East Gippsland weather district. Car access off Princes Highway 20 km W of Cann River.

The scenic drive along Euchre Creek Valley, once part of Princes Highway, passes through a gully of warm-temperate rainforest so dense in places that the nearby creek is totally obscured from view. Kanooka, blackwood and lilly pilly tower above an understorey of tree ferns and vines, with striking displays of wildflowers in spring and scattered crimson splashes of Gippsland waratahs in summer.

Highway realignment in the early 1960s has made a peaceful haven of the 1160 ha park and its creek-side rest area. A 4 km walking trail climbs away from picnic grounds along a ridge to the new highway, where a tall eucalypt forest dominated by silvertop ash overlooks the speeding traffic.
BEST TIME: Spring to autumn.
ENQUIRIES: (051) 58 6351.
ADDRESS: As for Alfred.

Scenic enjoyment ✓✓
Day activities ✓
Family camping ✗
Hard bushwalking ✗

Little Desert National Park
365 km NW, 8 km S of Kiata. Wimmera weather district. Car access of Western Highway at Kiata.

Soils unsuited to 19th-century agriculture gave the Little Desert its name, but average annual rainfalls of 400 mm support a variety of vegetation types. Sandy plains dominated by mallee and stringybark eucalypts extend west through the 35 300 ha park from woodlands of river red gum and black box on the Wimmera River flood plains. Smooth-barked yellow gums grow on isolated clay pans, and patches of reddish soils among the sand dunes foster broombrush and stringybarks.

Heath plants growing with the mallee produce impressive displays of wildflowers in winter and spring, attracting nomadic birds such as lorikeets and honeyeaters. Over 200 native bird species have been sighted in the park, including malleefowl. Its abandoned nesting mounds of sand and litter can be seen on one of the short nature trails that have been developed to sample the park's distinctive features.
NOTE: Water is scarce – visitors should carry their own.
BEST TIME: Spring (for wildflowers) and autumn.
ENQUIRIES: (053) 89 9218.
ADDRESS: RMB 389, Nhill 3418.

Scenic enjoyment ✓
Day activities ✓
Family camping ✓✓
Hard bushwalking ✓

Lower Glenelg National Park
400 km SW, 40 km NW of Portland. Western weather district. Car access off Princes Highway or Portland-Nelson road.
DESCRIPTION: Page 104.
NOTES: Bookings required for all camping in park. Fee charged for campsites and cabins at Caves camping ground.
VISITOR CENTRE: Princess Margaret Rose Caves, open daily.
BEST TIME: Spring (for wildflowers) to autumn.
ENQUIRIES: (087) 38 4051
ADDRESS: C/o P.O., Nelson 3292.

Scenic enjoyment ✓✓✓
Day activities ✓✓✓
Family camping ✓✓✓
Hard bushwalking ✓

Mitchell River National Park
300 km E, 60 km NW of Bairnsdale. East Gippsland weather district. Car access off Princes Highway via Fernbank.

This new national park of 11 900 ha, declared in 1986, incorporates the former Glenaladale National Park. The extension puts the focus in the park on the Mitchell River gorge which has some of Gippsland's most spectacular scenery.

The Den of Nargun, a rocky cave figuring in Aboriginal legends, stretches across the deep rainforest gully of Woolshed Creek as it descends to the steep, rapids-strewn gorge of Mitchell River. The creek may dry in summer, but when flowing it veils the 20 metre wide cave mouth with a fine curtain of water falling to a pool 3 metres below. Stalactites hang from the dripping roof and tall stalagmites grow to met them from the cave floor.

The steep-sided gully protects a warm-temperate rainforest of tall kanookas, pittosporums and lilly pillies shading a mass of ferns, orchids and tangled wood vines. Away from the cool humidity of the gully, drier soils in the park support magnificent stands of kurrajong, silvertop and box trees.

Short walking trails encircle the creek in one corner of the park, taking in a lookout bluff and branching off north along the Mitchell River below steep reddish cliffs. The park has some of the best white-water canoeing in Victoria.
NOTES: Limited camping – sites in gorge are restricted to canoeists and walkers in transit; bookings recommended. Licence required for fishing. Fires permitted only in authorised fireplaces.
BEST TIME: Year-round.
ENQUIRIES: (051) 52 6277.
ADDRESS: CFL Bairnsdale Region, 210 Main Street, Bairnsdale 3875.

Scenic enjoyment ✓✓
Day activities ✓✓
Family camping ✗
Hard bushwalking ✓

Morwell National Park
165 km SE, 16 km S of Morwell. West Gippsland weather district. Car access off Midland Highway between Churchill and Boolarra.

Rapid subdivision and development in surrounding forests in the 1960s prompted the former owner of Morwell to offer it for conservation. Gullies and ridges covering 280 ha in the southern foothills of the Strzelecki Ranges were not totally untouched, but one of the last patches of natural Gippsland forest was in good condition. In particular the area is a habitat of the rare butterfly orchid *Sarcochilus australis*, a small tree-clinging plant that in summer sends out a drooping stem clustered with yellow-green flowers distinguished by a tongue of red and yellow markings. The orchid grows on sheltered trees in gullies where southern blue gums and mountain grey gums tower over tree ferns and tall shrubs.

One of the two short walking trails established around the main gully climbs to ridges and spurs dominated by stringybark forest in the park's western section.
BEST TIME: Spring and early summer (for wildflowers).
ENQUIRIES: (051) 22 1478.
ADDRESS: Box 19, Churchill 3842.

Scenic enjoyment ✓✓
Day activities ✓
Family camping ✗
Hard bushwalking ✗

Mount Buffalo National Park
320 km NE, 96 km SE of Wangaratta. Northeast weather district. Car access off Ovens Highway at Porepunkah. Vehicle entrance fee.

PARKS OF THE MELBOURNE REGION

DESCRIPTION: Page 99.
NOTES: Bookings required for campsites during holidays. Camping ground closed late May to early November. Licence required for fishing. Cars must carry chains in winter; radiators need anti-freeze. Motel, lodge and guesthouse accommodation available.
WARNING: Severe weather changes occur suddenly throughout the year.
VISITOR CENTRE: Keown Lodge, open in summer and over Easter.
BEST TIME: Year-round (winter for skiing).
ENQUIRIES: (057) 55 1466.
ADDRESS: Mount Buffalo 3745.

Scenic enjoyment ✓✓✓
Day activities ✓✓✓
Family camping ✓✓✓
Walking, climbing ✓✓✓

Mount Eccles National Park
335 km W, 42 km S of Hamilton. Western weather district. Car access off Hamilton-Port Fairy road at Macarthur.
DESCRIPTION: Page 105.
NOTES: Fee charged for campsites; bookings required at Easter. Special facilities are available for disabled people.
BEST TIME: Spring and autumn.
ENQUIRIES: (055) 76 1014.
ADDRESS: RMB 1160, Macarthur 3286.

Scenic enjoyment ✓✓
Day activities ✓✓
Family camping ✓
Walking ✓

Mount Richmond National Park
390 km SW, 33 km W of Portland. Western weather district. Car access off Portland-Nelson road.
 Swamps and wet heathland around the base of Mt Richmond (229 metres) are fed by water that has seeped down through the hill's sandy soil and porous core. It is a hardened cone of volcanic ash, dust and pumice, covered by wind-blown sands from the shifting dunes of Discovery Bay. Rainwater sinks in instead of running off the surface to form streams.
 Correas, heaths, wattles and bush peas are well suited to these conditions. Over 400 flowering plants have been recorded in the 1700 ha park, providing impressive displays of wildflowers year-round, but particularly in spring.
 Walking tracks allow visitors the fullest access to heathlands and swamp areas and to the summit of Mt Richmond, where a lookout platform towers over forests of brown stringybark and manna gum for views of coastal and inland scenery.
BEST TIME: Spring (for wildflowers).
ENQUIRIES: (055) 23 3232.
ADDRESS: CFL Portland Region Office, Port and Heath Roads, Portland 3305.

Scenic enjoyment ✓✓
Day activities ✓✓
Family camping ✗
Hard bushwalking ✗

Organ Pipes National Park
25 km NW. Central weather district. Car access off Calder Highway at Sydenham. Train Melbourne-Sydenham (3 km from park).
DESCRIPTION: Page 84.
BEST TIME: Year-round.
ENQUIRIES: (03) 390 1082.
ADDRESS: C/o P.O., Diggers Rest 3427.

Scenic enjoyment ✓✓
Day activities ✓✓
Family camping ✗
Hard bushwalking ✗

Otway National Park
200 km SW, 14 km S of Apollo Bay. Western weather district. Car access off Great Ocean Road. Bus Melbourne-Apollo Bay.
DESCRIPTION: Page 80.
NOTES: Visits to Cape Otway lighthouse must be pre-arranged.
BEST TIME: Spring to autumn.
ENQUIRIES: (052) 37 6889.
ADDRESS: Box 63, Apollo Bay 3233.

Scenic enjoyment ✓✓✓
Day activities ✓✓
Family camping ✓✓✓
Hard bushwalking ✓✓✓

Port Campbell National Park
270 km SW. Western weather district. Great Ocean Road passes through park between Princetown and Peterborough.
DESCRIPTION: Page 103.
NOTES: Fee charged for campsites; bookings required in holiday periods.
WARNING: Dangerous waves along shoreline below cliffs.
VISITOR CENTRE: Port Campbell.
BEST TIME: Late spring to autumn.
ENQUIRIES: (055) 98 6382.
ADDRESS: Tregea Street, Port Campbell 3269.

Scenic enjoyment ✓✓✓
Day activities ✓✓✓
Family camping ✓✓✓
Hard bushwalking ✗

Snowy River National Park
450 km E, 135 km NE of Lakes Entrance. East Gippsland weather district. Car access along Bonang road off Buchan-Jindabyne road; turn off Princes Highway at Nowa Nowa for Buchan.
 Diversion and flow regulation in the upper reaches of the Snowy River have reduced the frequency of both flooding and drought along the river's deep valley. But heavy rains still cause sudden rises in the water level, particularly in gorges south of Mackillop Bridge, where the Snowy enters this 26 200 ha park. Boulders strewn across narrow passages become dangerous white-water rapids demanding great skill and endurance for canoeists. Trips from Mackillop Bridge take 3-4 days to the Buchan River junction.
 Walkers also follow the Snowy Valley south, but at Tulloch Ard Gorge the river is pinched between rock walls towering over a surging torrent. Hikers must be prepared to swim through the gorge to continue farther south. Less daunting walks include the Silver Mine Track, from Mackillops Bridge, which leads to an old mining area and provides scenic views of the Snowy River.
BEST TIME: Summer and autumn.
ENQUIRIES: (0648) 8 0277.
ADDRESS: As for Cobberas-Tingaringy.

Scenic enjoyment ✓✓✓
Day activities ✓
Family camping ✓
Walking, canoeing ✓✓✓

Tarra-Bulga National Park
195 km SE, 43 km S of Traralgon (Bulga 190 km SE, 38 km S of Traralgon). West Gippsland weather district. Car access off Princes Highway at Traralgon.
DESCRIPTION: Page 92.
NOTE: No camping in park.
BEST TIME: Year-round.
ENQUIRIES: (051) 96 6127.
ADDRESS: Balook via Yarram 3971.

Scenic enjoyment ✓✓✓
Day activities ✓✓
Family camping ✗
Hard bushwalking ✗

The Lakes National Park
300 km E, 60 km E of Sale. East Gippsland weather district. Car access via Longford and Loch Sport off Princes Highway at Sale. Rotamah Island accessible by boat, or on foot along Ninety Mile Beach.
 Long sandspits, low sand islands and the narrow stretch of dunes along Ninety Mile Beach, pushed up in the past 9000 years, enclose what was previously an immense bay in the Gippsland Lakes area. River silts have partly filled it, dividing it into a chain of freshwater lakes which could break out into Bass Strait only after exceptional flooding. But after a navigation channel was cut near Lakes Entrance in 1889, the level of the lakes fell by almost half a metre and the waters became brackish. Salt-marsh plants have colonised the widened lake margins, backed by paperbark scrublands, heaths and low woodlands of banksias and eucalypts.
 Although relatively remote by road from a string of nearby holiday towns, the natural bushland of the 2400 ha park is only a short boat trip away. Facilities for picnics and camping are generous. A bird hide at Lake Killarney, on one of the many walking tracks, allows visitors to study black swans, pelicans, grebes, ducks and cormorants without disturbing their feeding and breeding.
NOTES: Fee charged for camping at Emu Bight. Bookings required for camping in holidays.
BEST TIME: Spring to autumn.
ENQUIRIES: (051) 46 0278.
ADDRESS: C/o P.O., Loch Sport 3851.

Scenic enjoyment ✓✓
Day activities ✓✓✓
Family camping ✓✓✓
Hard bushwalking ✗

Wilsons Promontory National Park
230 km SW, 62 km S of Foster. West Gippsland weather district. Car access off South Gippsland Highway.
DESCRIPTION: Page 87.
NOTES: Fee charged for all camping. Campsites must be booked for holiday periods. Permit required for bush camping; numbers strictly limited. No wood fires November to April. Lodges and cabins also available.
VISITOR CENTRE: Tidal River.
BEST TIME: Spring to autumn.
ENQUIRIES: (056) 80 8538.
ADDRESS: Tidal River, via Foster 3960.

Scenic enjoyment ✓✓✓
Day activities ✓✓✓
Family camping ✓✓✓
Hard bushwalking ✓✓✓

Wonnangatta-Moroka National Park
340 km NE, 140 km N of Sale. North East weather district. Car access of Heyfield-Mansfield road at Licola.
 High peaks of the Great Dividing Range dominate the northern part of this 107 000 ha park and create a watershed for scores of rivers and streams which cut deep valleys and narrow gorges through the surrounding plateau of high snow plains. Strictly controlled grazing is allowed in certain limited areas and will be phased out elsewhere in 1991. Selective logging in forests of mountain gum and alpine ash is permitted until 1988. Neither activity interferes much with the enjoyment of bushwalkers, ski tourers, deer hunters, trout anglers and four-wheel-drive enthusiasts, for whom the rugged terrain has long been a popular destination.
NOTE: Licences required for fishing and deer hunting.
WARNING: Severe weather changes occur suddenly.
BEST TIME: Year-round (winter for cross country skiing).
ENQUIRIES: (051) 74 6166.
ADDRESS: CFL Traralgon Region, 71 Hotham St, Traralgon 3844.

Scenic enjoyment ✓✓✓
Day activities ✓
Family camping ✗
Hard bushwalking ✓✓✓

Wyperfeld National Park
450 km NW, 100 km N of Dimboola. Mallee weather district. Car access off Henty Highway at Hopetoun.
 Camping ground and short nature walks are centred on a chain of dry lakes that fill only on rare occasions when the Wimmera River floods north through the vast, sandy park. Mature stands of river red gum and black box lining the old watercourses testify to past floodings; their seeds will not germinate without plentiful ground moisture.
 Most of the 100 000 ha park, however, is dominated by vegetation types adapted to little change from their semi-arid conditions. Heaths grow on isolated claypans; sandy ridges support tea-trees, mallees and cypress pines.
NOTES: Permits required for bush camping. Fee charged for camping sites. Fires permitted only in authorised fireplaces. Carry drinking water on all walks in park.
BEST TIME: Midwinter and spring.
ENQUIRIES: (053) 95 7221.
ADDRESS: RMB 1465, Yaapeet 3424.

Scenic enjoyment ✓
Day activities ✓
Family camping ✓✓
Hard bushwalking ✓✓

Victoria's wildlife

More than any other state Victoria is dominated by high country. But as it sweeps south to the coast from the Alps and the semi-arid grasslands of the northwest it takes in many different types of landscape and habitat – high plains, great rock outcrops, temperate rainforest, heathlands, mallee, fern-filled gullies. Because of these varied environments it also has a wide range of plants and wildlife.

Platypus – receptors in the sensitive skin of the bill tell it about the underwater surroundings

Mountain pygmy-possum – may store seed as a food reserve for the alpine winter

Wallaroo – shaggy dark grey hair differentiates it from the western subspecies

Common wombat – in summer this forest-dweller seldom emerges from its burrow except at night

Little penguins – wait until dark before coming ashore in groups to roost in crevices or burrows

Australian shelduck – also known as the mountain duck, it prefers lowland areas and lives by brackish lakes

Brush-tailed rock wallaby – the soles of its thickly padded feet have rough granulations for grip; the tail is an essential element in balance

Malleefowl – the male is responsible for maintaining the mound nest and keeping it at the right temperature

Victoria's birds and flowers

Australian king parrot – feeds among the outer branches of forest trees, particularly on eucalypts and acacias

Flame robin – coats the outside of its cup-shaped nest with cobwebs or dry moss

Superb lyrebird – has a powerful voice that is unmatched for repertoire and mimicry

Australian pelican – groups sometimes swim slowly in formation to drive fish into the shallows

Grampians National Park *has almost 900 species of flowering plants, seen at their best from August to November. Among the orchids are: l, small helmet orchid; cl, slaty helmet orchid; b, mayfly orchid*

Shrubby velvet bush

Grampians thryptomene

Common heath – state emblem

Many of Baw Baw's summer hiking tracks become touring routes for cross-country skiers in winter

Cycling in thin winter sunshine on the nature drive at Wyperfeld

A walk in the fresh air to spark the appetite and then a sizzling sausage from the barbecue

Paddling along a tidal river in Wilsons Promontory National Park

Visitor activities in the national parks of Victoria

Bird watching
Churchill, Little Desert, The Lakes (special bird hides).

Bush camping
Baw Baw, Bogong, Brisbane Ranges, Cobberas-Tingaringy, Croajingolong, Grampians, Mitchell River, Otway, Snowy River, Wilsons Promontory.

Bushwalking
Alfred, Baw Baw, Bogong, Brisbane Ranges, Churchill, Cobberas-Tingaringy, Croajingolong, Fern Tree Gully, Fraser, Grampians, Kinglake, Lind, Little Desert, Lower Glenelg, Mitchell River, Morwell, Mount Buffalo, Mount Eccles, Mount Richmond, Organ Pipes, Otway, Port Campbell, Snowy River, Tarra-Bulga, The Lakes, Wilsons Promontory, Wonnangatta-Moroka.

Camping
Fraser, Grampians, Kinglake, Little Desert, Lower Glenelg, Mount Buffalo, Mount Eccles, Otway, Port Campbell, Snowy River, The Lakes, Wilsons Promontory, Wonnangatta-Moroka.

Canoeing/boating
Cobberas-Tingaringy, Croajingolong, Fraser, Grampians, Lower Glenelg, Mitchell River, Mount Buffalo, Otway, Snowy River, The Lakes, Wonnangatta-Moroka.

Car touring and 4-W driving
Baw Baw, Bogong, Brisbane Ranges, Cobberas-Tingaringy, Croajingolong, Grampians, Snowy River, Wonnangatta-Moroka.

Cave tours
Lower Glenelg.

Cycling
Bogong, Churchill, Fern Tree Gully, Wilsons Promontory.

Deer hunting
Wonnangatta-Moroka.

Fishing, ocean
Cape Schanck, Croajingolong, Otway, Port Campbell, The Lakes, Wilsons Promontory.

Fishing, freshwater
Baw Baw, Cobberas-Tingaringy, Croajingolong, Fraser, Grampians, Little Desert, Lower Glenelg, Mitchell River, Otway, Snowy River, Wilsons Promontory, Wonnangatta-Moroka.

Geological studies
Mount Eccles.

Croajingolong, with its wide variety of plant, animal and bird life in inland areas, and its great stretches of unspoiled coastline, is magnificent territory for hikers

Historical studies
Brisbane Ranges, Port Campbell.

Horse riding (in specified areas)
Baw Baw, Bogong, Cape Schanck, Cobberas-Tingaringy, Grampians, Kinglake, Lower Glenelg, Mount Buffalo, Snowy River, Wonnangatta-Moroka.

Photography
Alfred.

Picnicking
Alfred, Baw Baw, Bogong, Brisbane Ranges, Cape Schanck, Churchill, Croajingolong, Fern Tree Gully, Fraser, Grampians, Kinglake, Lind, Little Desert, Lower Glenelg, Mitchell River, Morwell, Mount Buffalo, Mount Eccles, Mount Richmond, Organ Pipes, Otway, Port Campbell, Tarra-Bulga, The Lakes, Wilsons Promontory.

Power boating
Fraser, Lower Glenelg, Wilsons Promontory.

Orienteering
Churchill.

Rafting, white water
Cobberas-Tingaringy, Mitchell River, Snowy River.

Rock climbing
Grampians, Mount Buffalo.

Scenic driving
Lind, Mount Buffalo, Otway, Port Campbell, Tarra-Bulga, Wilsons Promontory.

Skiing, cross country/downhill
Baw Baw, Bogong, Cobberas-Tingaringy, Mount Buffalo, Wonnangatta-Moroka.

Scuba diving
Wilsons Promontory.

Snorkelling
Wilsons Promontory.

Surfing
Cape Schanck, Otway, Wilsons Promontory.

Swimming
Cape Schanck, Cobberas-Tingaringy, Croajingolong, Fraser, Grampians, Mount Buffalo, Port Campbell, Snowy River, Wilsons Promontory.

Tobogganing
Mount Buffalo.

Walking along coastal tracks and beaches
Cape Schanck, Croajingolong, Otway.

Water skiing
Fraser, Lower Glenelg.

Wildflower studies
Brisbane Ranges, Churchill, Grampians (best area in Victoria), Little Desert, Mount Richmond – all outstanding in spring.

Windsurfing
Fraser.

Yachting
Fraser, The Lakes, Wilsons Promontory.

CAMPING
Bush camping — away from it all, no facilities other than those you create.
Camping — a pit toilet and a tap but no other facilities.
Family camping — established camping ground with showers, toilets, barbecue areas and where you can probably take a caravan, but check beforehand.

There is good beach fishing from many of the state's national parks

Launceston & Devonport regions

Reminders of an age when ice ruled the land

ALPINE SCENERY presents its boldest face in the Tasmanian highlands. Peaks and bluffs towards the north coast stand in sharper relief than any to be seen on the mainland Great Divide. Their craggy profiles were carved by glaciers about 20 000 years ago, during the last ice age. Creeping rivers of ice chewed at the flanks of brittle dolerite outcrops. The debris formed moraines that now pen high lakes, or it slipped into valleys to make stony wastelands of their floors. Boulders dragged over the central plateau gouged holes to be filled by hundreds of glittering tarns.

Even now, in a climate far milder, winter frosts crack more rock and spring thaws move the rubble down the slopes. Alpine heaths and gnarled, low-growing shrubs have to withstand months under snow. And visitors must beware of the onset of severely cold, wet weather at any time of year.

Launceston and Devonport, northern Tasmania's principal entry points for air travellers and car-ferry traffic respectively, have ready access to the most arresting mountain scenery. The state's best skifields, on the high massif of Ben Lomond, are only 50 km from Launceston. In summer the moorlands are an untracked wilderness of flowering heaths, and the 'organ pipe' dolerite columns of the surrounding bluffs make an unforgettable sight.

Outstanding examples of glaciated landforms are concentrated at Cradle Mountain, two hours or so from Devonport. Peaks in the national park – or the Reserve, as Tasmanians often call the district – create a jagged skyline above lakes of icy clarity and deeply carved, rock-strewn valleys. A picture-postcard snow scene in winter, it has a bleak majesty all its own after the thaw.

In contrast to the nearby highlands, easily accessible parks on the north coast enjoy mild climates and markedly lower rainfall, but they lack much scenic distinction. Freycinet, even more sheltered and sunny on the east coast, offers the greatest diversity in its peaks and sea cliffs of granite and its long white beaches. But motorists will see little: Freycinet is a park for walking and boating.

Mainlanders visiting any of the national parks in these regions – except Ben Lomond and Cradle Mountain in the winter sports season – will notice an unusual freedom from population pressures. Traffic is light and facilities are seldom over-used. Natural surroundings can be appreciated in northern Tasmania with the least likelihood of human distraction.

Featured parks	Pages
❶ Ben Lomond	122-123
❷ Freycinet	124-125
❸ Cradle Mountain-Lake St Clair	126-127
❹ Rocky Cape	128-129
❺ Hellyer Gorge	130-131

Your access and facilities guide to every national park in these regions starts on page 132

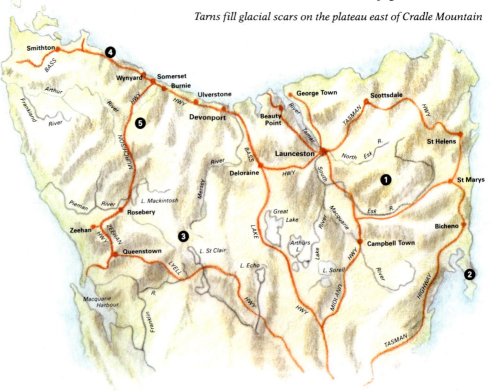

Tarns fill glacial scars on the plateau east of Cradle Mountain

Frost-resistant plants cling precariously in thin soils capping each column of dolerite. The rock was formed in the same way as columnar basalt, from the cooling of magma that intruded into sedimentary rock. But it is less rich in silica, and more than 100 million years older than most basalts found on the mainland

BEN LOMOND NATIONAL PARK

Half an hour from Misery Bluff, cross-country skiers reach the Plains of Heaven. Pressing on, they find Little Hell. Ben Lomond's lofty plateau, bristling with the colourful names beloved of skiers, is Tasmania's premier snow-sports area. A commercial alpine resort perches on the flanks of the tallest peak, Legges Tor (1572 metres). Out of season the 16 500 ha park offers adventure – without marked trails – to walkers and climbers prepared to brave a chilly climate. Deep beds of dolerite, bared by eons of erosion of overlying sedimentary rock, were smashed and scoured by the movement of glaciers in the last ice age. Above 1250 metres, frost action is still breaking down the rock. Gravity moves the debris into valleys where it builds blockfields – barren or sparsely vegetated areas where chunks of rock cover a layer of peat. But the alpine moors are fertile: creeping cushion plants appear through melting snow, and heaths flower brilliantly in summer. Celery-top pine and a stunted, deciduous beech called tanglefoot – both peculiar to Tasmania – grow at sub-alpine levels, above eucalypt woodlands.

Broken rock slides down the flanks of Stacks Bluff (1527 metres) on the southernmost edge of the plateau. Glaciers tore at the dolerite columns for thousands of years. Now frost carries on the destruction, shrinking and cracking the rock

An icy dawn breaks over moorlands between Lake Youl (foreground) and Lake Baker. Far to the east are the peaks of the Tower Hill Range

LAUNCESTON AND DEVONPORT REGIONS 123

Freycinet National Park

Roads reach only 6 km into a mountainous park of nearly 11 000 ha. Visitors prepared to continue on foot find tracks winding over or round the four-peaked ridge of the Hazards to a low, marshy isthmus bordered by Hazards Beach and Wineglass Bay – each with a campsite. A circuit of the Hazards can be made in half a day. To the south, hardy walkers can traverse most of the western coast of Freycinet Peninsula and its high central spine, dominated by Mt Freycinet (620 metres). The full round trip takes two days, with a camp at Cooks Beach to break the journey. Schouten Island, accessible only by boat, has a camp but no tracks. Coastal scrubs and heaths, flowering profusely in spring, make up most of the vegetation. Birds and small marsupials are abundant.

Schouten Island, seen from the south between Taillefer Rock and Freycinet Peninsula, is split by a clear faultline. The near side consists of mostly bare granite; timbered heights beyond were formed separately, from dolerite. Left: To the north of the peninsula, the steep faces of the Hazards jut into Thouin Bay. Mt Dove (485 metres) is on the left

Granite cliffs (left) line Lemon Bight at Cape Forestier, on the northeastern corner of Freycinet Peninsula. The coastline veers sharply westward to Wineglass Bay (above), where swampy heathlands back a waterline walking route. Swimming can be dangerous from the eastern side of the park, exposed to Tasman Sea swells. Sandy beaches on the opposite side, fronting Great Oyster Bay, are safe and highly popular in late summer

Cradle Mountain's dolerite peaks tower over the icy waters of Lake Dove

A slow-moving sheet of ice covered this plateau between 20 000 and 15 000 years ago. The glacier tore rocks from the flanks of outcrops such as Barn Bluff (background); dragged along in the ice, they gouged out countless hollows that are now lakes and tarns

Cradle Mountain–Lake St Clair National Park

Mountain scenery of stark, unforgettable grandeur unfolds itself to walkers with a week or more to spare for the north-south traverse of Tasmania's most famous park. The going is fairly easy on the Overland Track, but side-track climbs are much harder. And bitter weather can strike at any time – warm clothing and waterproofs should be carried. Many shorter walks, taking about half a day, are available on tracks starting near the access roads at each end of the 132 000 ha park.

In the north, Cradle Mountain and Barn Bluff dominate a landscape of open moors and heathlands, dotted with lakes and tarns. Peaks ringing the park's central plain include Mt Ossa, Tasmania's tallest at 1617 metres. Valleys to the south, squeezed between the Du Cane and Traveller Ranges, funnel into the long, deep basin of Lake St Clair, which is the source of Hobart's River Derwent.

Vegetation ranges from beech rainforests to alpine grasses, snow gums and ancient species of pines. Wildlife includes echidnas, platypuses, marsupial 'cats', Tasmanian devils and wombats.

Sailing boats can be launched into Lake St Clair

Tiny beaches at Rocky Cape gain shelter from tongues of tough quartzite reaching into Bass Strait. Waters are usually calm and safe to the east of the cape but the area has one notable shipwreck – an early steamer that lost its way in blinding bushfire smoke

Rocks off the cape are tilted almost vertically from their original bedding planes. The district has a complicated history of earth movements involving folding, faulting, tilting, dolerite intrusion and volcanic eruptions, along with glacial striation – the scratching effect of boulders dragged in ice

ROCKY CAPE NATIONAL PARK

Silver banksia

Cassinia (right), one of the paper daisies, and coast tea-tree (below) cope well on poor, sandy soils. Common heath (bottom right), widespread from NSW to SA, was first found at Rocky Cape

Wooded slopes of the Sisters Hills back a jagged coastline littered with reefs and islets and pitted with water-worn caves. Aborigines used some of the caves for at least 8000 years: archeological interest was the chief reason for the park's proclamation in 1967. Remains from the feasting of generations of hunters and seafood gatherers can be seen in two caves open to the public near the western end of Sisters Beach, and in two more on Flagpole Hill, at Rocky Cape itself.

Easy, well-marked walking trails cover most of the 3000 ha park. Some lead to little pocket beaches between headlands jutting into Bass Strait; rock pools and crevices hold a fascinating range of marine life. Other tracks climb the hills, where two lookouts offer impressive coastal views. Scrubs and flowering heaths are dominant but the inner slopes have peppermint eucalypts and patches of stringybark forest. Sea eagles, roosting on promontories and in some of the taller trees, are among more than 90 bird species seen in the park.

Scented paperbark

Orchids growing on the bark of old rainforest trees beside the Hellyer River

Flood-worn boulders border a cascading tributary stream

Tree ferns (above) and epiphyte fishbone ferns (below) grow densely in the wet gorge

HELLYER GORGE

Chilling rains are frequent in the steeply winding gorge of the Hellyer River. But given any luck with the weather, travellers on the lonely Murchison Highway south from Somerset could find no more delightful wayside stop. A state reserve of 570 ha straddles the road each side of the Hellyer Bridge, offering picnic grounds screened by big tree ferns. A short but sometimes slippery track leads to the river through a rainforest of tall myrtle beech, encrusted with mosses, fungi and epiphyte orchids. Similar forests once covered hills to the north and east, now planted with exotic trees. Swift-running streams feed the Hellyer, which is itself a major tributary of the Arthur River, the most important waterway of northwestern Tasmania. Henry Hellyer, an explorer-surveyor for the Van Dieman's Land Company, made the first European ascent of Cradle Mountain in 1831.

PARKS OF THE LAUNCESTON AND DEVONPORT REGIONS

FACILITIES

 Cabins
 Caravan park
 Equipped picnic area
 Bush camping allowed
Lavatory building

Established campsite
Campsite but no car access

Note: Popular parks without campsites usually have public camping grounds nearby. If in doubt, call enquiries number.

PARK RATINGS No interest ✗ Some interest ✓ Major interest ✓✓ Outstanding ✓✓✓

Asbestos Range National Park
60 km NW of Launceston, 40 km E of Devonport. Central North and Midlands weather district. Car access from Launceston on West Tamar Highway and Badger Head Road, or from Devonport on Frankford Road and Bakers Beach Road. Approach roads gravel.

Coastal heathlands merge into dry eucalypt woodlands in a park of nearly 4300 ha extending from Port Sorell to Greens Beach, on the western edge of Port Dalrymple. Two long, sandy beaches are separated by the humped mass of Badger Head. Swimming is popular at both, though the western end of Bakers Beach has strong currents.

Many easy walks can be taken on the coast or into the foothills of the Asbestos Range. A hide for waterfowl observation is provided at a freshwater lagoon behind Bakers Beach, half an hour's walk from a car park. Birds of the heaths and woodlands are also abundant. Wallabies and wombats are particularly common and forester kangaroos, which died out here last century, have been successfully reintroduced.

BEST TIME: Spring to autumn.
ENQUIRIES: (004) 28 6277.
ADDRESS: NPWS head office, Box 210, Sandy Bay 7005.

Scenic enjoyment ✓
Day activities ✓✓✓
Family camping ✓✓
Hard bushwalking ✗

Ben Lomond National Park
50 km SE of Launceston. East Coast weather district. Car access on Launceston-Ben Lomond road. Entrance fee in ski season. Risky bends on ascent to ski village; chains should be carried in winter. Snowfalls may close road. Buses from Launceston in ski season.

DESCRIPTION: Page 123.
NOTE: Alpine resort accommodation privately arranged through Northern Tasmanian Alpine Club.
BEST TIME: Skiing June-September, walking November-April.
ENQUIRIES: (003) 41 5312 or (003) 99 3414 (ski season only).
ADDRESS: As for Asbestos Range.

Scenic enjoyment ✓✓✓
Day activities ✓
Family camping ✗
Hard bushwalking ✓✓✓

Cradle Mountain-Lake St Clair National Park
85 km S of Devonport. Central Plateau and Upper Derwent Valley weather district. Car access to Cradle Valley end via Forth or Gowrie Park; last 30 km gravel. Snowfalls may close road. Lake St Clair end accessible by car or bus from Hobart (170 km) on Lyell Highway to Derwent Bridge.

DESCRIPTION: Page 127.
NOTE: Fees charged for hut use and for the Overland Track.
WARNING: Severe weather possible even in summer. Walkers should register plans with ranger.
BEST TIME: November-March.
ENQUIRIES: Northern end (003) 63 5187, southern end (002) 89 1115.
ADDRESS: As for Asbestos Range.

Scenic enjoyment ✓✓✓
Day activities ✓
Family camping ✓
Hard bushwalking ✓✓✓

Freycinet National Park
180 km SE of Launceston. East Coast weather district. Car access via Lake Leake and Coles Bay. Car and bus access from Hobart (200 km) via Tasman Highway. Entrance fee.

DESCRIPTION: Page 124.
NOTE: Camp bookings required midsummer, Easter.
WARNING: Carry water on longer walks.
BEST TIME: Summer-autumn.
ENQUIRIES: (002) 57 0146.
ADDRESS: Via Coles Bay 7215.

Scenic enjoyment ✓✓
Day activities ✓✓✓
Family camping ✓✓✓
Hard bushwalking ✓✓

Hellyer Gorge State Reserve
100 km W of Devonport. Northwest Coast weather district. Murchison Highway from Somerset passes through reserve.

DESCRIPTION: Page 131.
BEST TIME: Spring to autumn.
ENQUIRIES: (003) 41 5312.
ADDRESS: As for Asbestos Range.

Scenic enjoyment ✓✓✓
Day activities ✓
Family camping ✗
Hard bushwalking ✗

1. **Asbestos Range NP**
2. **Ben Lomond NP**
3. **Cradle Mountain-Lake St Clair NP**
4. **Freycinet NP**
5. **Hellyer Gorge State Reserve**
6. **Mount William NP**
7. **Rocky Cape NP**
8. **Strzelecki NP**
9. **Walls of Jerusalem NP**

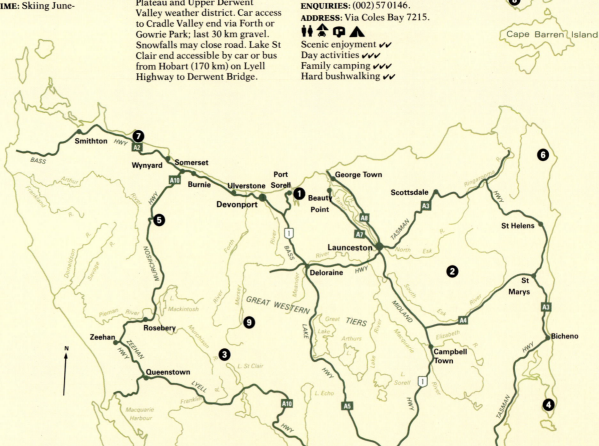

PARKS OF THE LAUNCESTON AND DEVONPORT REGIONS

THE OVERLAND TRACK:
Cradle Mountain-Lake St Clair

Enough sidetracks to keep hikers and climbers occupied for weeks lead off the 80 km trail linking craggy Cradle Mountain with forested hills around the placid expanse of Lake St Clair. Walks of five days or more sample diverse moorland, mountain and gorge landscapes.

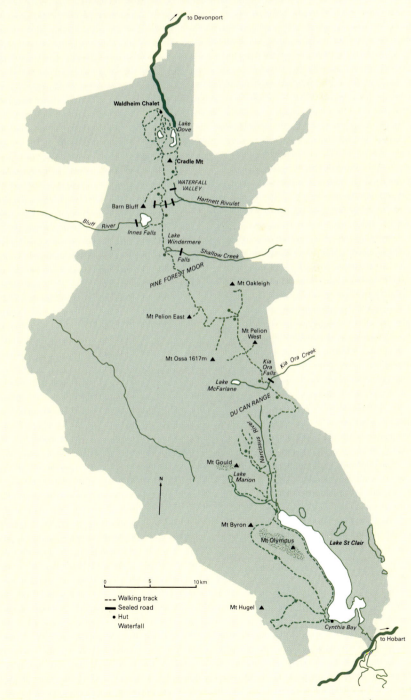

Mount William National Park
160 km E of Launceston. Northeast weather district. Car access via Tasman Highway and Herrick-Gladstone road; unsealed roads in park.

Long, open bays each side of Cape Naturaliste have sandy beaches popular for swimming and fishing. Dunes and coastal heathlands in a park of nearly 14 000 ha contrast with timbered inland slopes leading up to Mt William (216 metres) and Baileys Hill. They make up the biggest protected area of dry eucalypt forest in Tasmania.

The park is managed principally as a wildlife reserve, giving sanctuary to forester kangaroos, Bennett's wallabies, echidnas, pademelons, wombats, marsupial 'cats' and Tasmanian devils. Seabirds are abundant along with scores of forest and heath species.
NOTE: Bore water available near campsites.
BEST TIME: Summer.
ENQUIRIES: (003) 57 2108.
ADDRESS: As for Asbestos Range.

Scenic enjoyment ✓
Day activities ✓✓
Family camping ✓✓
Hard bushwalking ✓

Rocky Cape National Park
100 km W of Devonport. Northwest Coast weather district. Car access via Bass Highway, turning off for Sisters Beach 12 km past Wynyard, or Rocky Cape 30 km past Wynyard. Burnie-Stanley buses pass park.
DESCRIPTION: Page 129.
BEST TIME: November-March.
ENQUIRIES: (003) 41 5312.
ADDRESS: As for Asbestos Range.

Scenic enjoyment ✓
Day activities ✓✓
Family camping ✗
Hard bushwalking ✓

Strzelecki National Park
165 km NE of Launceston. Northeast and Flinders Island weather district. Air access only: Launceston-Whitemark daily, Hobart-Whitemark Mon., Wed., Fri. Cars, bicycles for hire – 7 km to park entrance.

Granite peaks of the Strzelecki Range, topped by Mt Strzelecki (800 metres), dominate a park of 4200 ha at the southwestern corner of Flinders Island. The area is mostly undeveloped but a track leads up to the mountain to reveal excellent views of the island and others in the Furneaux group. The climb takes 4 hours.

Behind coastal heathlands are slopes of dry eucalypt forest and valleys supporting dense stands of moisture-loving species such as blue gums and peppermints. Tree ferns are prolific in some gullies. Wildlife does not differ markedly from mainland Tasmania but a local wombat, classed as a subspecies, is smaller and softer-furred than the usual type and more active by day.
BEST TIME: Summer.
ENQUIRIES: (003) 59 2148.
ADDRESS: As for Asbestos Range.

Scenic enjoyment ✓✓
Day activities ✓✓
Family camping ✓✓
Hard bushwalking ✓✓

Walls of Jerusalem National Park
110 km W of Launceston, 115 km S of Devonport. Central Plateau and Upper Derwent Valley weather district. Car access on Bass Highway to Deloraine, then via Mole Creek and Mersey Forest road (unsealed).

Sheer dolerite cliffs rise forbiddingly to the northwest of the central plateau – what Tasmanians call the Lake Country. In the lower valleys of the 11 500 ha park, groves of pencil pines surround glacier-carved lakes and tarns, and grassy expanses are decked with wildflowers in early summer. Sub-alpine heaths and wet grasslands share the plateau. Gnarled snow gums cling to rocky ridges near the Walls. A big population of marsupials includes wallabies, potoroos, wombats, possums and native 'cats'. Parrots are prominent in a wide variety of birds.

A well-defined walking track ascends to the plateau from the Fish River. It penetrates the Walls through Herod's Gate and passes Lake Salome at the base of the tallest cliff, West Wall (1490 metres). Mt Jerusalem (1458 metres) stands not far south. Two shelter huts are provided. Rock climbers find ample opportunities, and parts of the plateau in winter are suited to cross-country skiing.
WARNING: Sudden changes of weather.
BEST TIME: Summer.
ENQUIRIES: (003) 41 5312.
ADDRESS: As for Asbestos Range.

Scenic enjoyment ✓✓✓
Day activities ✗
Family camping ✗
Hard bushwalking ✓✓✓

LAUNCESTON AND DEVONPORT REGIONS 133

CONFRONTATION

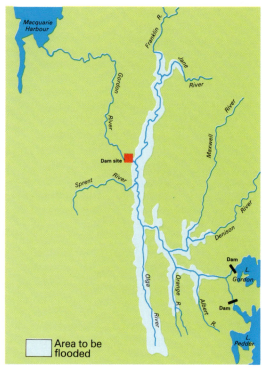

Waters backing up from the dam would have flooded 37 km of the Gordon Valley, 33 km of the Franklin Gorge, and parts of seven tributaries. The power station was to have had an average annual output of 172 megawatts. The whole scheme was expected to take 9½ years at a cost of $136 million, with a peak workforce of 1200

How the west was won

TASMANIA'S Gordon River dam conflict redrew the battle lines of environmental debate in Australia. What started in 1980 as yet another 'greenie' protest ended three years later in a constitutional showdown that changed the face of federal-state relations. Along the way, 1272 opponents of hydro-electric exploitation of the western rivers were arrested and 447 were imprisoned. But the real casualties were politicians.

'No Dams' campaigners drew strength from their frustration a decade earlier, when the pent-up waters of Lake Pedder engulfed a national park. Opposition marshalled then – too late – formed the nucleus of the Tasmanian Wilderness Society. Knowing that the next target of power generation planning would be the Gordon River, and that the Franklin would probably be involved as a major tributary, the society built its case well in advance. Films and photographs were assembled to depict the wild beauty of the two rivers and their gorges. Lectures and publications were prepared. Mainland and international support was enlisted.

Late in 1979 the state Hydro-Electric Commission proposed a dam on the Gordon immediately below its junction with the Franklin, flooding the valleys of both rivers and part of seven others. A power station 1 km downstream would meet Tasmania's estimated needs for the rest of the century. Other possibilities were more expensive and less productive. With both of the state's major political parties wedded to cheap power as a way to industrial growth, the HEC seemed certain to win again.

But local and national dissent was mobilised on an unprecedented scale in 1980. The Australian Heritage Commission placed the Tasmanian wilderness on its register of the National Estate. Yielding, the Labor state cabinet chose an alternative: the Gordon would be dammed higher up, at its junction with the Olga River. The Franklin, untouched, would be the focus of a new Wild Rivers National Park. The state's upper house, however, insisted on the HEC's Franklin scheme.

Fresh force was lent to the anti-dam argument in 1981 by the discovery that caves along the wild rivers, crammed with Aboriginal artefacts, had been occupied before and during the glacial phase of the last ice age. By then the government was committed to resolving its parliamentary deadlock by referendum. Premier Douglas Lowe was deposed and his successor, Harry Holgate, presided over a poll in which the only formal choice was one dam or other. A third of voters spoiled their ballots – most wrote 'No Dams' – but a clear majority consented to drowning the Franklin.

Early in 1982 the federal government nominated the western Tasmanian wilderness parks for World Heritage listing. But the state Liberal opposition leader, Robin Gray, claimed that he was assured of commonwealth loan funding for the power scheme. The Holgate government fell and the Liberals enjoyed a record success at the ensuing elections. Laws were quickly passed to start the dam project and to revoke parts of Wild Rivers National Park needed by the HEC. And in anticipation of physical confrontations, the police were given the power of on-the-spot arrest for trespass.

On the mainland, a Tasmanian application to have the World Heritage nomination withdrawn was rejected by the federal government. The Labor opposition caucus formally opposed any damming in western Tasmania –

contradicting the state ALP policy. In an outer-Melbourne by-election 40 per cent of voters wrote 'No Dams'. In Paris the World Heritage listing was proclaimed. That signalled the start of the active blockade. Executing a long-hatched plan, protesters swarmed into the west to obstruct HEC site preparation and the movement of equipment. Their quixotic exploits, and the soaring toll of arrests, were chronicled daily in the national media.

Late in January 1983 Prime Minister Malcolm Fraser offered $500 million to finance a coal-fired power station instead of the hydro project. Premier Gray refused, and Mr Fraser repeated that his government could not intervene against the state's will. A few days later he called a general election. Labor under Bob Hawke won a sweeping victory, and quickly passed regulations forbidding HEC activities in the World Heritage area. On 1 July 1983 the High Court confirmed that the federal government's World Heritage obligations entitled it to override state powers. A year later the Tasmanian government accepted a compensatory offer from Canberra of $277 million.

Blockaders wait in a picket line of inflatable dinghies to challenge barges bringing bulldozers up the Gordon River. More than 2600 people signed up to take part in the blockade, which lasted nearly three months. Charges against those arrested – and often jailed for not accepting bail conditions – were eventually dropped

HOBART REGION

Seaside splendour and a challenging wilderness

EVEN IN the heart of Tasmania's capital, lonely landscapes are evoked. The River Derwent draws its flow from sources as far-flung as the northern Great Lakes, the glacier-chiselled central plateau, the chilling depths of Lake St Clair and the forested ranges west towards Mt Field. On their way to Hobart these waters drive the turbines of a dozen power stations – symbols of the conflict between industrialisation and conservation that splits Tasmanian society.

Downstream, the broadening Derwent estuary is shielded from Storm Bay by a hooked string of ridged peninsulas, unconvincingly linked by low sandspits. The same formation occurs again and again around the wilder coast beyond: Bruny Island, Tasman and Forestier Peninsulas, Maria Island, Freycinet Peninsula. At the lip of Storm Bay, Cape Raoul defies the Tasman Sea with jagged walls of dolerite. They signify the colossal upsurge of magma under half of Tasmania, emerging after eons of surface weathering to give it a special look.

Crags of dolerite even cap Mt Wellington, 1270 metres above the city's western outskirts. From the Pinnacle lookout tourists see not only the winding course of the Derwent and the intricacies of the coast, but also a seemingly endless series of timbered ranges receding to the west. The untamed southwest virtually starts here, above Hobart.

That fact was brought home savagely to city people in 1967, when bushfires swept over and round the mountain; 51 lives were lost and factories and hundreds of homes were destroyed.

Mt Field, the national park most accessible from the capital, is also the best in the range of forest and alpine plant communities it has on show in a relatively small area. Parks and reserves to the east of Hobart offer striking coastal scenery and ample opportunity for maritime diversions. Lake Pedder, vastly enlarged to the horror of ecologists, makes an aquatic playground in the northern part of Southwest National Park.

Few people other than the most determined walkers and climbers experience more of Southwest, or much of Wild Rivers National Park. Together these two, and Cradle Mountain-Lake St Clair, constitute a true wilderness of a size and quality that thoroughly merit its World Heritage listing. Here adventurers find Australia's best rafting rivers and its most celebrated system of mountain-and-ocean walking trails. The principal route, spanning 180 km from Lake Pedder to Port Davey on the west coast and around to Catamaran in the far south, is a trudge of at least eight days. The reward is a matchless variety of unspoilt scenes.

Featured parks	Pages
❶ Wild Rivers	138-141
❷ Southwest	142-143
❸ Mount Field	144-145
❹ Maria Island	146-147
❺ Tasman Peninsula	148-149
❻ Truchanas Reserve	150

Your access and facilities guide to every park in this region is on page 151

Dolerite clusters 165 million years old confront the ocean at Cape Raoul

On Frenchman's Cap, in the Deception Range, a glacier-cut quartzite face rising 300 metres challenges rock climbers

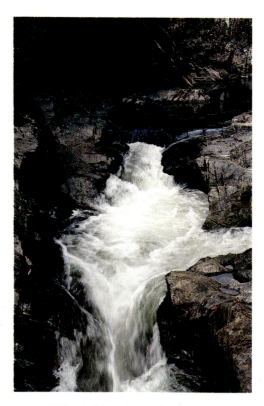

Grass triggerplants grow on lower forest slopes

Shiny tea-tree occurs in the rockiest areas

High rainfall in the catchment ranges keeps tributaries such as the Alma River (above) running full year-round to supply the Franklin (right). Myrtle beech crowds the steep flanks of the Franklin Gorge, which offers canoeists and rafting parties the longest white-water adventure in Australia

Wild Rivers National Park

'No Dams' confrontations and political ructions in the early 1980s made Gordon and Franklin household names. But few Australians see these rivers, let alone their catchment ranges. Franklin-Lower Gordon Wild Rivers National Park covers nearly 200 000 ha of midwestern Tasmania. It links two older parks, Cradle Mountain-Lake St Clair and Southwest, and absorbs a third, Frenchman's Cap, to complete a continuous band of high-country wilderness with a westward arm down the Gordon to the coast at Macquarie Harbour.

Rainforests are dominated by myrtle beech but they contain some Huon pine. There are eucalypt forests on drier slopes as well as high heaths, buttongrass plains and boglands. Scores of bird species nesting in the park include the endangered orange-bellied parrot. Possums are the most prominent marsupials, but Tasmanian devils and native 'cats' may also be seen at night.

Boats from Strahan take scenic cruises up the lower Gordon, and motorists on the Lyell Highway can sample the upper Franklin bush along a 2 km track starting 4 km south of the Collingwood bridge. Deeper penetration of the park, by raft or canoe or by hard walking and climbing, should be attempted only by seasoned and well-equipped parties in consultation with rangers.

Near the end of its journey to Macquarie Harbour, the Gordon River takes a tortuous course through the Elliott Range

Wild Rivers National Park

Nectar from leatherwood (left) makes a celebrated honey. Other forest shrubs include lomatia (above) and daisy bush (right)

Below: Buttongrass makes a natural meadow on moist ground north of Frenchman's Cap

Celery-top, King Billy and Huon pines fringe the Franklin River while young plants colonise a sand bar

Quartzites and schists of the Arthur Range were twisted and folded eons ago, then jaggedly carved by glacial action during the last ice age

Southwest National Park

Lake Pedder's lucid waters, raised in the early 1970s for hydro-electric storage, swallowed one national park but became the centrepiece for another, far bigger. Embracing the enlarged lake, the 440 000 ha of Southwest reach out beyond the Frankland and Arthur Ranges to the west and south coasts through a wilderness of rocky ridges and deep, forested valleys. Visitors restricted to car travel can reach the northwestern and southeastern shores of the lake, where boating and trout fishing are popular. Swimming is possible but the water is always cold. The rest of the park poses stern tests for the most serious bushwalkers and climbers. Tracks radiating from an access route south of the lake reach Port Davey and other points on a rugged, lonely coast.

Precipitous Bluff (1120 metres) presents a challenge to rock climbers in the far south of the park. Dense rainforests of myrtle beech surround the outcrop. Southwest also has extensive alpine moorlands of heath and stunted scrub, and buttongrass meadows at lower levels

Mount Field National Park

Towering examples of *Eucalyptus regnans*, the world's tallest hardwood, guard the entrance to an astonishing kingdom of trees. The road in winds from 100 metres above sea level to more than 1000. Moorlands and ridges climb still higher beyond Lake Dobson, culminating in Mt Field West (1434 metres). Every type of inland Tasmanian tree community is represented in a park of 17 000 ha: rainforest species, varied stands of eucalypts and stunted alpine scrubs. Curiosities include wind-bent 'horizontal scrub', the bane of bushwalkers, and pandani, the world's tallest heath. It grows to 9 metres and looks more like a palm. *Athrotaxis*, a genus of conifers peculiar to Tasmania, grows in two widely different forms, King Billy and pencil pine.

Bird and animal life is as diverse as the plants. Half of all Tasmania's bird species have been seen here. Furtive, nocturnal marsupials may include the thylacine or Tasmanian tiger – the last in captivity was trapped nearby in the 1930s.

Contrasting nature walks can be taken from the road to Russell Falls, just inside the park, and at two points higher up. A further easy track encircles Lake Dobson. Steep slopes just west of the lake are popular skifields in winter. Snow usually lies on the high moors until November. Cross-country ski trails lead west and north. After the thaw, strenuous walks taking up to a day each way are available. But rainfall is high throughout the year and bitterly cold snaps are frequent.

Mountain heath

Below: *Dicksonia tree ferns – 'manferns' – frame Russell Falls*

Filmy fern colonises mossy spots on rotting logs

Gentianella favours wet alpine soils

Eucalypts and pines share the shores of Lake Dobson

Left: Eucalyptus regnans *can exceed 100 metres in height. Widely known as mountain ash, here it is called swamp gum – and its timber is sold as Tasmanian oak*

HOBART REGION 145

Sea caves are forming in jointed limestone at Pyramidal Rock, Cape Maurouard. Similar cliffs to the north at Cape Boullanger contain marine fossil deposits of great scientific importance

Below: Heath-clad ridges on McRae's Isthmus, above the sands of Shoal Bay, are old beaches – formed when the sea level was higher or the land lay lower

Sedimentary deposits from four or five successive geological periods are revealed by erosion of the island's raised eastern edges. The lowest beds are about 400 million years old

Two steep, forested masses linked by a low isthmus provide visitors with peaceful walks and a stiff climb to Mt Maria (709 metres). Much of the sheltered western shore, facing Mercury Passage, is lined with sandy beaches where swimming and boating are popular in summer. Dry eucalypt forests cover most of the slopes, but there are also open heathlands and some ferny creek gullies. The quick progression of habitats, from shoreline to sub-alpine, gives an island of less than 10 000 ha an unusual wealth of bird species. Prominent mammals include forester kangaroos and Bennett's wallabies – not endemic to the island but put there to ensure the survival of their kind.

Maria Island National Park

TASMAN PENINSULA

Storm-torn bluffs and cliffs, reaching for 25 km down the eastern side of Tasman Peninsula, present travellers on the approach to Eaglehawk Neck with the most arresting view of a wild coast to be seen in all Australia. Famous features such as the Tessellated Pavements, the Blowhole, Tasman's Arch and the Devil's Kitchen are within easy reach near the isthmus. Farther afield over forested hills, eroded clusters of columnar dolerite form extraordinary sea cliffs. They are equally impressive at Cape Raoul (page 380), Cape Pillar and Cape Hauy, where some columns stand needle-like offshore. Sheltered beaches are found south of Port Arthur and in Fortescue Bay, north of Cape Hauy. A scenic walking track between Fortescue and Waterfall Bays takes six hours each way.

Boulders carried by an ancient glacier are embedded in the sedimentary layers of a bluff at Fortescue Bay. Grooves in the face indicate a recent collapse, through undercutting by wave action

Tidal erosion of a shore platform at the northern end of the Eaglehawk Neck isthmus has exaggerated the cracks between blocks of vertically jointed sandstone. The tiled appearance inspired their name: the Tessellated Pavements

Truchanas Reserve

The finest known stand of fully developed Huon pine forest survives in a reserve of 400 ha, named for the Lithuanian migrant who saved it. Most other forests had disappeared by the middle of last century, felled for their strong, rot-resistant but easily worked timber. A few trees remain scattered in riverside rainforests of the west and southwest, but rarely are they fully grown and dominant. Those of the reserve are at least 1000 years old, and bear feathery tops up to 40 metres high.

After their discovery by a Denison River rafting party in 1928, they were safe for 40 years – too remote for profitable logging. But the enlargement of Lake Pedder brought them closer to transport routes. Olegas Truchanas, a leading bushwalker and conservationist, foresaw the threat and succeeded in having the reserve proclaimed in 1970. He was killed two years later, canoeing the Gordon River.

Huon pines dominate a forest on gentle slopes west of the Denison River, where seedlings thrive on floodplain soils. Found only in Tasmania, the tree was classed as Dacrydium *until 1984, when botanists agreed to change its name to* Lagarostrobus franklinii

PARKS OF THE HOBART REGION

Hartz Mountains National Park
85 km SW. West and South Coast and Highlands weather district. Car access off Huon Highway from Geeveston via Arve Road and Hartz Road. Last 15 km gravel; can be closed by snow.

Easy access from the Huon Valley makes this a popular park for weekend walkers and day visitors from Hobart. A high spine of dolerite peaks, running north-south between the catchments of the Arve and Picton Rivers, dominates an area of 6500 ha. The highest point, Hartz Peak, is 1255 metres. Winter snowfalls make cross-country skiing possible. Glacial moraines hold six attractive lakes on the flanks of the range.

Beech rainforests around the Keogh Falls and Arve Falls, near the park entrance, give way to tall eucalypt forests and finally to alpine moorlands where heaths are interspersed with snow gums. Short, easy walks can be taken to the falls or to lakes at the end of the road. A further track (2 hours each way) leads on to Hartz Lake or Hartz Peak.

WARNING: Area subject to sudden storms, mists; take waterproofs and warm clothing.
BEST TIME: Year-round (winter for cross-country skiing, late spring for wildflowers).
ENQUIRIES: (002) 30 8033.
ADDRESS: NPWS head office, Box 210, Sandy Bay 7005.

Scenic enjoyment ✓✓✓
Day activities ✓✓
Family camping ✗
Hard bushwalking ✓✓

Maria Island National Park
100 km NE, 15 km SE Triabunna. East Coast weather district. Ferry from Louisville resort; air charters from Triabunna. Cars not allowed on island.
DESCRIPTION: Page 147.
NOTES: No shops on island; no water at Encampment Cove. Camp bookings needed. Take own cooker. Itineraries for longer walks should be registered with ranger.
BEST TIME: Spring to autumn.
ENQUIRIES: (002) 57 1420.
ADDRESS: As for Hartz Mountains.

Scenic enjoyment ✓✓
Day activities ✓✓
Family camping ✓✓
Hard bushwalking ✓

Mount Field National Park
75 km W. West and South Coast and Highlands weather district. Car access via Lyell Highway and Maydena road. Chains needed in winter; snow may close park road. Buses from Hobart Mon.-Sat.
DESCRIPTION: Page 144.
NOTE: Camp and cabin bookings needed during summer. Self registration system operates at other times. Submit extended walk plans to ranger.
Facilities for handicapped people – including Russell Falls track.
BEST TIME: Summer-autumn (winter for skiing).
ENQUIRIES: (002) 88 1149.
ADDRESS: As for Hartz Mountains.

Scenic enjoyment ✓✓✓
Day activities ✓✓
Family camping ✓✓✓
Hard bushwalking ✓✓✓

Southwest National Park
160 km W. West and South Coast and Highlands weather district. Car access via Lyell Highway and Gordon River Road. Route sealed to Strathgordon, gravel to Scotts Peak Dam. Entrance fee.
DESCRIPTION: Page 142.
NOTES: Facilities shown are just outside park. Long walking plans must be registered with rangers or police.
BEST TIME: Spring, late summer-autumn.
ENQUIRIES: (002) 88 1283.
ADDRESS: As for Hartz Mountains.

Scenic enjoyment ✓✓✓
Day activities ✓✓
Family camping ✓✓✓
Hard bushwalking ✓✓✓

Tasman Peninsula State Reserves
80 km SE. Southeast weather district. Car access via Arthur Highway to Port Arthur.
DESCRIPTION: Page 148. Ten areas are protected as state reserves under NPWS control. Facilities shown are widely dispersed; only the Lime Bay camp is in a reserve.
NOTE: Swimming safest at Lime Bay, Pirates Bay, Stewarts Bay.
BEST TIME: Spring to autumn.
ENQUIRIES: (002) 50 2107.
ADDRESS: As for Hartz Mountains.

Scenic enjoyment ✓✓✓
Day activities ✓✓
Family camping ✓✓
Hard bushwalking ✓✓

Truchanas Nature Reserve
200 km W. West and South Coast and Highlands weather district. No vehicle access. Hard walking over Hamilton Range from Strathgordon (30 km); Denison River access by raft.
DESCRIPTION: Page 150.
BEST TIME: Summer.
ENQUIRIES: (002) 30 8033.
ADDRESS: As for Hartz Mountains.

Scenic enjoyment ✓✓✓
Day activities ✗
Family camping ✗
Hard bushwalking ✓✓✓

Wild Rivers National Park
200 km NW, 42 km SE Queenstown. West and South Coast and Highlands weather district. Car access via Lyell Highway. Queenstown buses pass entrance. Boat access to lower Gordon River from Strahan.
DESCRIPTION: Page 139.
BEST TIME: Summer.
ENQUIRIES: (004) 71 7122.
ADDRESS: As for Hartz Mountains.

Scenic enjoyment ✓✓✓
Day activities ✓✓
Family camping ✗
Hard bushwalking ✓✓✓

FACILITIES: Cabins, Caravan park, Equipped picnic area, Bush camping allowed, Lavatory building, Established campsite, Campsite but no car access.

Note: Popular parks without campsites usually have public camping grounds nearby. If in doubt, call enquiries number.

PARK RATINGS No interest ✗ Some interest ✓ Major interest ✓✓ Outstanding ✓✓✓

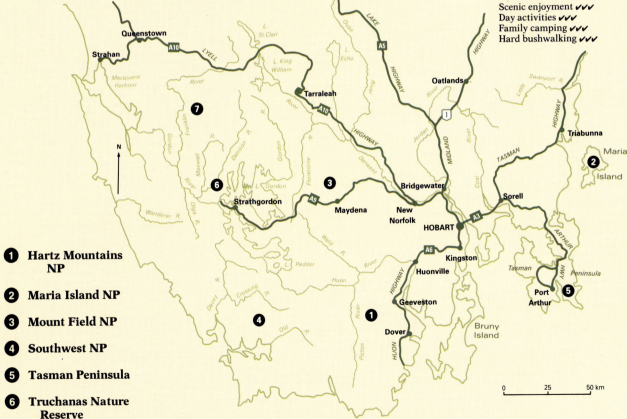

1. Hartz Mountains NP
2. Maria Island NP
3. Mount Field NP
4. Southwest NP
5. Tasman Peninsula
6. Truchanas Nature Reserve
7. Wild Rivers NP

Plants in Tasmania's parks

Cut off from the mainland quite recently, in geological time, Tasmania is a world of its own. Developing in isolation, some of its plants and animals are unique, while others have developed differently from their mainland relations. Still others are all that remain of species which once flourished in other states. In its World Heritage area is one of the world's last great temperate wildernesses. Because of the wealth of trees and water, forest species of animals and plants are abundant; in summer the coastal heathlands attract birdlife – honeyeaters, scrub wrens pink robins and others busy themselves among the tea-tree and flowering plants.

Although it looks tropical, Richea pandanifolia is a heath unique to Tasmania. Growing to 12 metres it is one of the world's tallest

Glow-worms' sticky threads trap food

Horizontal scrub initially grows vertically but then bends under its own weight

Bellendena montana, mountain rocket, another Tasmanian native

Correa reflexa, the native fuchsia

Diplarrena moraea is a member of the iris family

Pink robins inhabit the undergrowth and fern-filled gullies of temperate rainforest

Hairy leek orchid

Broad-lip leek orchid,

Tasmanian birds and animals

Sugar gliders can volplane about 50 metres

The long-nosed potoroo is highly variable in size and colour, depending on where it is found

Still common in northern and eastern Tasmania, the eastern barred bandicoot has almost disappeared elsewhere

Busy grey fantails greeted by a hungry chorus line of newly fledged chicks

Bennett's wallaby, a subspecies of the red-necked wallaby, has longer, denser fur and a different breeding cycle

The Tasmanian form of common brushtail possum is larger, woollier and darker than on the mainland

In winter the Tasmanian pademelon uses its forepaws to uncover vegetation buried under snow

Blue-winged parrots blend so well with the background that they are difficult to see when foraging among grasses

Most of the Tasmanian population of striated pardalotes crosses Bass Strait to winter on the mainland

155

Visitor activities in the national parks of Tasmania

Abseiling
Freycinet.

Bird watching
All national parks.

Bush camping
All national parks.

Bush walking
All national parks.

Camping
All national parks.

Canoeing/boating
Asbestos Range, Freycinet, Maria Island, Mount William, Rocky Cape, Southwest, Strzelecki, Wild Rivers.

Car touring
Asbestos Range, Ben Lomond, Mount Field, Mount William, Rocky Cape, Southwest.

Fishing, ocean/beach
Asbestos Range, Freycinet, Maria Island, Mount William, Rocky Cape, Southwest, Strzelecki.

Fishing, freshwater
Cradle Mountain-Lake St Clair, Mount Field, Walls of Jerusalem.

Geological studies
Ben Lomond, Cradle Mountain-Lake St Clair, Freycinet, Hartz Mountains, Maria Island, Mount Field, Rocky Cape, Southwest, Strzelecki, Walls of Jerusalem, Tasman Arch and Blowhole.

Historical studies
Historic sites and Maria Island.

Horse riding
Asbestos Range, Mount William.

Orienteering
Asbestos Range, Ben Lomond, Cradle Mountain-Lake St Clair, Freycinet, Hartz Mountains, Maria Island, Mount Field, Mount William, Rocky Cape, Strzelecki, Wild Rivers.

Photography
Asbestos Range, Tasman Arch and Blowhole.

Picnicking
Asbestos Range, Hellyer Gorge, Tasman Arch and Blowhole, Walls of Jerusalem.

Power boating
Asbestos Range, Freycinet, Maria Island, Mount William, Rocky Cape, Strzelecki.

Rafting
Wild Rivers.

Eddystone Lighthouse in Mount William National Park was built in 1889. It is sometimes open to visitors

Rock climbing
Ben Lomond, Cradle Mountain-Lake St Clair, Freycinet.

Skiing, cross country/downhill
Ben Lomond, Cradle Mountain-Lake St Clair, Mount Field, Walls of Jerusalem.

Scuba diving
Freycinet, Maria Island, Mount William, Rocky Cape, Strzelecki.

Snorkelling
Asbestos Range, Freycinet, Maria Island, Mount William, Rocky Cape, Strzelecki.

Surfing
Mount William.

Swimming
Asbestos Range, Cradle Mountain-Lake St Clair, Freycinet, Maria Island, Mount William, Rocky Cape, Strzelecki.

Tobogganing
Ben Lomond, Mount Field.

Walking along coastal tracks and beaches
Asbestos Range, Freycinet, Maria Island, Mount William, Rocky Cape, Southwest, Strzelecki, Tasman Arch and Blowhole.

Hartz Mountains in winter: in spring and summer the moorlands are a sea of wildflowers

Dense forests in the lower levels of Mount Field National Park contrast with the sparse shrub cover above the treeline where a ski area has been developed

Day walking near Lake Pedder in Southwest National Park

Southwest, largest of the parks, is mostly remote wilderness where small, fully equipped walking parties camp out to get to know and understand the state's great forests and the creatures that live in them

Mount William has sweeping beaches for riding or walking and the waters offshore provide good fishing

Water skiing
Asbestos Range, Freycinet, Mount William, Rocky Cape.

Wildflower studies
All national parks.

Wildlife observation
Asbestos Range, Cradle Mountain-Lake St Clair, Freycinet, Maria Island, Mount Field, Mount William.

Windsurfing
Asbestos Range, Freycinet, Maria Island, Mount William, Rocky Cape.

Yachting
Asbestos Range, Cradle Mountain-Lake St Clair, Freycinet, Maria Island, Mount William, Rocky Cape, Strzelecki.

CAMPING

Bush camping — away from it all, no facilities other than those you create.

Camping — a pit toilet and a tap but no other facilities.

Family camping — established camping ground with showers, toilets, barbecue areas and where you can probably take a caravan, but check beforehand.

INDEX

Bold numerals indicate major illustrated entries; italics indicate other illustrations

A

Aboriginal sites *43*, 64, *107*, 129, 134
Acacias 21, 24-7
Adelaide 46
Alfred 23, 110
Alligator Creek 56
Alma River *138*
Anakie Gorge *79*
Angular pigface *62*
Ants, harvester 27
Artesian water 16
Arthur Range 142
Arthur River 131
Asbestos Range 132
Ash, mountain 24, *144*, *145*
Athrotaxis pines 144
Atmospheric pressure 12

B

Balconies *107*
Bales Beach 55
Banksias 24, 27, *129*
Baobab *21*
Barn Bluff *127*
Basalt 10, *15*
Bass Strait 12, 14, *80*, *85*, *128*
Bat, ghost *39*
Baw Baw 110
Beach formation 18-19
Beech 22-3
 myrtle *22*, *92*, *138*, *143*
 negrohead *22*, *23*
 tanglefoot *123*
Beetle, leaf-eating *25*
Belair 67
Ben Lomond 120, **122-3**, 132
Black sands *18*
Black-eyed Susan *55*
Bogong 77, **100-1**, 110
Bogong High Plains *40*
Bogong Plateau 100
Brigalow 25
Brisbane Ranges 77, **78-9**, 110
Broken Falls *109*
Buffalo Plateau 99
Bulga (*see* Tarra-Bulga)
Bunyeroo Valley *60*
Burrowa-Pine Mountain 110
Bush pea *79*
Bushfire 34-5, *97*, 137
Buttongrass *140*

C

Calder River 80
Camels 27
Canunda 46, **64-5**, 67
Cape Banks 64
Cape Boullanger 146
Cape Buffon 64
Cape Forestier *125*
Cape Hauy 148
Cape Maurouard *146*
Cape Otway 80
Cape Pillar 148
Cape Raoul *136*, 148
Captain James Cook (*see* Croajingolong)
Cassinia *129*
Casuarinas 24, 27

Catamaran 137
Cats, feral 41
Cave formations 104
Celery-top pine *141*
Chalka Creek 95
Churchill 110
Climate 10, 12, 16, 20-1
Coast tea-tree *129*
Coasts and islands 18-19
Cobberas-Tingaringy 111
Coffin Bay 46, **62**, 67
Conifers 20
Continental drift 20
Cooks Beach 124
Coorong 46, **66**, 67
Coral 10, *18*
Coral fern *90*
Cradle Mountain-Lake St Clair 23, 34, 42, 120, *121*, **126-7**, 132, 133
Croajingolong 23, 77, **96-7**, 111
Crocodiles 35
Crystal Brook 98
Cyanophytes *20*
Cyathea Falls *92*, *94*
Cyathea tree fern *92*
Cycads 20, *21*

D

Daisies *26*, *99*, *129*
Daisy bush *140*
Damage to parks 31, 32, 36, 40-1
Dandenong Ranges 25
Deception Range *138*
Deep Creek 67
Deer 31
Denison River 151
Derwent River 16, 127, 137
Devil's Kitchen 148
Devonport 137
Dicksonia tree fern *144*
Dicksons Falls 99
Dieback 25
Distress signals 34
Dolerite *11*, *15*, *107*, *126*, *136*
Double-tails orchid *82*
Du Cane Range 127

E

Eaglehawk Neck 148, *149*
Eastern Highlands 11, 14-15, 16, 18, 20
Elliott Range *139*
Elliott River 80
Epacrids 27
Ephemeral plants 26
Epiphytes 22-3
Erosion 10-11, 14-15, 18-19
Eucalypts 21, 24-5
Eucalyptus regnans (*see* Mountain ash)
Eurobin Falls 99
Evaporation 12
Everlasting pea *49*
Everlastings *26*, *79*
Evolution of plants 20-1, 24-5
Eyre Peninsula 16, 62, 63

F

Falls Creek, 100
Feral animal damage 40-1, *59*
Fern Gully 92
Ferns
 coral *90*
 filmy *92*, *145*
 fishbone *131*
 kangaroo *93*
 see also Tree ferns
Fern Tree Gully *30*, 111
Figs 20, *23*
Filmy fern *92*, *145*
Fire 12, 21, 24-5, 34-5
Fishbone fern *131*
Flagpole Hill 129

Flat Rock Shelter *107*
Flinders Chase 46, **52-3**, 67
Flinders Ranges 15, 46, *47*, **58-61**, 67
Forests 20-5
Fortescue Bay *148*
Frankland Range 142
Franklin Gorge 134, *138*
Franklin River 42, 134-5, 138-9, *141*
Fraser 112
Fraser, Malcolm 135
Frenchman's Cap *138*
Freycinet 120, **124-5**, 132
Frog, gastric-brooding *38*, 39
Frost 12-13
Funnel-web spider 34

G

Gammon Ranges *15*, 67
Gentian, mountain *98*
Gentianella *145*
Geology 14-15
Ghost bat *39*
Gibson Steps 103
Glacial action *14*, 15, 120, *123*, *127*, *148*
Gleichenia (coral) fern *90*
Glenaladale (*see* Mitchell River)
Glenelg River *104*
Gneiss 10
Goat, feral *41*
Golden Island *62*
Golden-shouldered parrot *39*
Gondwanaland 10-11, 20, 22-23
Goodenia ovata 82
Gordon River 10, 134-5, 138-9
Gordon Valley 134
Grampians 76, 77, **106-9**, 112
Grand Canyon *107*
Granite 10-11
Grass trigger plant *138*
Grass-trees 27, *48*, *79*
Grasshopper, Leichhardt's *38*
Grasslands 21, 26
Gray, Robin 134
Great Artesian Basin 11, 16
Great Australian Bight 12, 18, 26, 62
Great Barrier Reef 42, 43
Great Divide 14
Great Dividing Range 12, 14, 16, 18, 27
Great Oyster Bay *125*
Greviliea 27, *78*, 79
Guinea flowers *55*
Gull, silver *66*
Gums
 mountain *98*
 river red *25*, *59*
 snappy *26*

H

Hairy cutleaf daisy *100*
Hairy-nosed wombat *38*
Halls Gap 106
Hartz Mountains 151
Hastings River mouse 38, *39*
Hattah-Kulkyne 36, 39, 46, **95**, 112
Hawke, Bob 135
Hazards *124*
Heat waves 12
Heathlands 27
Heaths 27, *100*, *129*, *144*
Hellyer, Henry 131
Hellyer River *130*, 131
Heritage Commission, Aust. 17, 43, 134
Heysen, Hans 46
Heysen Trail 46
Hobart 137
Holgate, Harry 134
Hop *26*
Hummock grasses *26*
Huon pine *141*, *150*
Hydro Electric Commission 134

I

Igneous rocks 10
Insect, sap-sucking *25*
Innes 67
Ironstone *53*
Island Arch *102*
Islands 19

J

Jackson's Creek 84
Jarrah 25
Jussieu Peninsula 63

K

Kakadu 16, *33*, *38*, 42, 43
Kangaroo fern *93*
Kangaroo Island 52-5
Kentbruck Heath 104
Kimberleys, WA 10, 12, 15, 16-17, 25
King Billy pine *141*, 144
Kinglake 77, **81-3**, 112
Kinglake Ridge 81
Koala *78*

L

Lake Albert 66
Lake Alexandrina 66
Lake Baker *123*
Lake Bonney 64
Lake Catani *99*
Lake Dobson 144, *145*
Lake Dove *126*
Lake Eyre 16, 68
Lake Pedder 134, 142
Lake St Clair 16, *127*
Lake Surprise *105*
Lake Youl *123*
Land Conservation Council 77
Landforms 10-11
Launceston 120
Leatherwood *140*
Leeches 35
Legges Tor 123
Leichhardt's grasshopper *38*
Lemon Bight *125*
Lignotubers 24, 26
Limestone 10
 caves 104
Lincoln 46, **63**, 68
Lind 112
Little Desert *16*, 39, 77, 112
Loch Ard Gorge 102-3
Lomatia *140*
London Bridge *103*
Lowe, Douglas 134
Lower Glenelg 77, **104**, 112

M

Macks Creek 92
Macquarie Harbour 139
Magnolias 20
Maits Rest 80
Mallacoota Inlet *97*
Mallee 26, *27*, *61*
Malleefowl *38*, 39, 77
Mallee Cliffs 111
Mambray Creek *56*
Mangroves 18
Maria Island 137, **146-7**, 151
McKenzie River *109*
McRaes Isthmus *146*
Melbourne 77
Mercury Passage 147
Metamorphic rock 10
Millstream palm *21*
Mitchell grass 26

158

Mitchell River 112
Moisture 12-13, 16-17
Moleside Creek *104*
Monsoon 12, 23
Morialta Creek 50
Mornington Peninsula 85
Morwell 112
Mosses 20
Mount Bishop 86
Mount Bogong 100
Mount Boulder 91
Mount Buffalo 77, **98-9**, 112
Mount Dove *124*
Mount Eccles 77, **105**, 113
Mount Field 23, 137, **144-5**, 151
Mount Freycinet 124
Mount Hotham 100
Mount Lofty 35, 46, 48
Mount Lofty Ranges 48, 50
Mount Maria 147
Mount Ossa 127
Mount Remarkable 46, **56-7**, 69
Mount Richmond 113
Mount Wellington 137
Mount William 106, 133
Mountain ash 24, 144, *145*
Mountain gentian *98*
Mountain gum *98*
Mountains 10-15
Mouse, Hastings River 38, *39*
Mulga 26, 27
Mungo 12, 16
Murray River 16, 25, 95
Musk daisy *82*
Myrtle beech 22, *92*, *138*, *143*

N
National Estate 43, 134
National park management 30-33, 35
Negrohead beech 22, *23*
Ninety Mile Beach *17*
Nobby Island *54*
Norman Bay 90
Numbat *38*
Nullarbor *27*, 69

O
Open forests 24-5
Orchids 23, 27, *82*, *84*
Organ Pipes 15, *41*, 77, **84**, 113
Otway 23, 77, **80**, 113
Otway Range *80*

P
Palms, distribution 20, 23
Pandani 144
Paper daisy *99*, *129*
Paperbarks 25, 27, *129*
Park worker 33
Parker River 80
Parrot, golden-shouldered *39*
Paterson's curse *49*
Pelican *66*
Pencil pine *20*, 144
Pets in parks 37
Phyllodes 26
Picnic Point 88
Pigface, angular *62*
Pigs, feral 41
Pimelea *63*
Pines
 celery-top *141*
 distribution 20
 Huon *141*, 150
 King Billy *141*, 144
 pencil *20*, 144
Planning a visit 37
Plant evolution 20-1, 24-5
Poached-egg daisy *26*
Point Avoid 62
Point Hicks *96*

Port Campbell 77, **102-3**, 113
Port Davey 142
Port Douglas 62
Port Lincoln 63
Possum, striped *39*
Powers of rangers 33
Precipitous Bluff *143*
Princess Margaret Rose Caves 104
Psyllids 25
Public participation 36
Pultenaea *56*
Purpose of national parks 30-1
Pyramidal Rocks *146*

Q
Quartzite 10, 15

R
Rainfall 12-13
Rainforests 22-3
Rangers 32-3
Redback spider 34
Refuge Cove 36
Regeneration 24-5
Restoration of parks 40-1
Rhyolite 10, 15
River red gum *59*
Rivers and lakes 16, *17*
Rock art *43*, *107*
Rock types 10, 14-15
Rocky Cape 120, **128-9**, 133
Rocky River 53
Rosette Rock 84
Rowsley Fault 79
Ruined Castle *101*
Russell Falls *144*

S
Safety and survival 34-5
Salt Creek 66
Saltbush *26*, *27*
Sand
 mining 40
 movement 18-19, *64*, *65*
 types 18
Sandstone 10
Sassafras *92*
Scented paperbark *129*
Schouten Island *124*
Scrublands *26*, *27*
Sea-eagle, white-bellied *55*
Sea lion *55*
Sedimentary rocks 10
Serra Range *106*
Shale 10
Sherbrooke River 103
Shiny tea-tree *138*
Shoal Bay *146*
Shores 18-19
Signalling for help 34
Silver gull *66*
Sisters Hills *129*
Slate 10
Snakebite 34
Snowy River 36, 113
Soft tree fern *93*
Soil types 15, 26-7
Solanum *60*
Southern Ocean 66
Southwest 23, *35*, *42*, 137, **142-3**, 151
Spider bites 34
Spinifex, coastal *26*, *96*
St Mary Peak *59*
Stacks Bluff *123*
Steiglitz grevillea *78*, 79
Stings and bites 34
Storm Bay 137
Storm Boy 66
Strahan 139
Strangler fig 23

Striped possum *39*
Strzelecki 133
Strzelecki Ranges 92
Sunshine 12
Survival and safety 34-5
Sydenham Inlet 97

T
Taillefer Rock *124*
Tanglefoot beech *123*
Tarra-Bulga 77, **92-4**, 113
Tasman's Arch *148*
Tasmanian tiger 39, 144
Taylors Landing 63
Tea-trees *129*, *138*
Temperature 12, 14
Templetonia retusa 63
Tessellated Pavement 84
Tessellated Pavements *149*
The Lakes 16, *17*, 113
Thistle Island *63*
Thouin Bay *124*
Thurra River 96
Thylacine (Tasmanian tiger) 39, 144
Tick bites 34
Tidal River *87*, *90*
Tides 18-19
Tower Hill Range *123*
Trachyte 10, 15
Trade winds 12
Traveller Range *127*
Tree evolution 20-1, 24-5
Tree ferns
 dicksonia *93*, *144*
 soft *93*
Truchanas, Olegas 150
Turtle 33
Tussock grasses 26-7, *60*
Twelve Apostles *103*

V
Vegetation 20-7
Vivonne Bay *54*
Volcanoes 10-11, 14-15, *105*
Voluntary park work 36

W
Walls of Jerusalem 23, 133
Wandoo 25
Waterfall Bay *148*
Waterfall Gully 48
Waterloo Bay *87*, *89-90*
Wave action 18-19
Weather patterns 12, *13*
Weeds 36, *49*, *84*
Wetlands 17
Whisky Bay *88*
Wilderness Society 36, 134
Wildlife conservation 38-39
Wild Rivers 23, *42*, 134-5, 137, **138-141**, 151
Willandra Lakes, NSW 16, 26, 42-3
Wilpena Pound *58-9*
Wilson Range 90
Wilsons Promontory *22*, *23*, 36, 77, **86-91**, 113
Wimmera River *16*
Winds 14
Wineglass Bay *124*, *125*
Wingan Inlet (absorbed – see Croagingolong)
Witjira 69
Wombat, hairy-nosed *38*
Wombelano Falls *82*
Wonnangatta-Moroka 113
Woodlands 21, 24-5
World Heritage List 42-3, 134-5
Wyperfeld *27*, *39*, 113

Y
Younghusband Peninsula 66

Z
Zierra *55*
Zircon, oldest *11*

OTHER FEATURED PARKS

Black Hill and Morialta Conservation Parks 46, **50-1**, 67
Cape Schanck Coastal Park 77, **85**, 110
Cleland Conservation Park 35, 46, **48-9**, 67
Hellyer Gorge State Reserve 120, **130-1**, 132
Naracoorte Caves Conservation Park 69
Seal Bay Conservation Park 46, **54-5**, 69
Tasman Peninsula State Reserves 137, **148-9**, 151
Truchanas Nature Reserve 137, **150**, 151

Protect our parks and wildlife

- Observe all fire bans.
- Use only fireplaces provided, or your own portable cooker.
- Don't take cats or dogs with you.
- Don't take firearms or other hunting weapons.
- Don't leave litter.
- Don't disturb or remove plants, rocks or animals.
- Obey 'No Entry' signs – they are for your safety, and also protect fragile areas.
- Keep your vehicle to formed roads and marked parking areas.

ADDRESSES

Park services

ACT Parks and Conservation Service
Box 158, Canberra 2601. (062) 46 2211

Australian National Parks and Wildlife Service
Box 636, Canberra City 2601. (062) 46 6211

Conservation Commission of the Northern Territory
Box 1046, Alice Springs 5750. (089) 50 8211

New South Wales National Parks and Wildlife Service
Box N189, Grosvenor Street P.O., Sydney 2000. (02) 237 6500

Queensland National Parks and Wildlife Service
Box 190, North Quay 4002. (07) 227 4111

Great Barrier Reef Marine Park Authority
Box 1379, Townsville 4810. (077) 81 8811

South Australian National Parks and Wildlife Service
GPO Box 1782, Adelaide 5001. (08) 216 7777

Tasmanian National Parks and Wildlife Service
Box 210, Sandy Bay 7005. (002) 30 8033

Department of Conservation Forests & Lands
240 Victoria Parade, East Melbourne 3002. (03) 651 4011

Department of Conservation and Land Management
Box 104, Como 6152. (09) 367 0333

Parks associations

National Parks Association of the Australian Capital Territory
Box 457, Canberra City 2601. (062) 57 1063

National Parks Association of New South Wales
275c Pitt Street, Sydney 2000. (02) 264 7994

National Parks Association of Queensland
GPO Box 1752, Brisbane 4001. (07) 870 8086

Nature Conservation Society of South Australia
310 Angas Street, Adelaide 5000. (08) 223 5155

Tasmanian Conservation Trust
GPO Box 684, Hobart 7001. (002) 34 3552

Victorian National Parks Association
285-287 Little Lonsdale Street, Melbourne 3000. (03) 663 3591

Conservation Council of Western Australia
794 Hay Street, Perth 6000. (09) 321 4507

Park foundations

New South Wales National Parks and Wildlife Foundation
GPO Box 2666, Sydney 2001. (02) 27 7971

National Parks Foundation of South Australia
98 Currie Street, Adelaide 5000

Australian Conservation Foundation
672b Glenferrie Road, Hawthorn 3122. (03) 819 2888

Australian Trust for Conservation Volunteers

Vic.: Box 412, Ballarat 3350. (053) 32 7490
WA: Box 100, Melville 6156. (09) 335 5508

National Trust of Australia

ACT: 71 Constitution Avenue, Campbell 2601. (062) 47 6766
NT: Box 3520, Darwin 5794. (089) 81 2848
NSW: Observatory Hill, Sydney 2000. (02) 27 5374
Qld: Old Government House, George Street, Brisbane 4000. (07) 229 1788
SA: Ayers House, 288 North Terrace, Adelaide 5000. (08) 223 1655
Tas.: 39 Paterson Street, Launceston 7250. (003) 31 9077
Vic.: 4 Parliament Place, Melbourne 3000. (03) 654 4711
WA: 4 Havelock Street, Perth 6000. (09) 321 6088

Wilderness Society

ACT: Box 188, Civic Square, Canberra 2608. (062) 49 8011
NSW: 57 Liverpool Street, Sydney 2000. (02) 267 7929
SA: Shop 44, Grote Street, Adelaide 5000. (08) 231 0625
Tas.: 130 Davey Street, Hobart 7000. (002) 34 9366
Vic.: 59 Hardware Street, Melbourne 3000. (03) 67 5229
WA: 794 Hay Street, Perth 6000

World Wildlife Fund Australia

GPO Box 528, Sydney 2001. (02) 29 7572

Environment centres

ACT: Childers Street Buildings, Kingsley Street, Canberra 2600. (062) 47 3064
NT: Box 2120. Darwin 5794. (089) 81 1984
NSW: 176 Cumberland Street, Sydney 2000. (02) 27 4206
Qld: 166 Ann Street, Brisbane 4000. (07) 221 0188
Tas.: 102 Bathurst Street, Hobart 7000. (002) 34 5566
Vic.: 285 Little Lonsdale Street, Melbourne 3000. (03) 663 1561
WA: 794 Hay Street, Perth 6000. (09) 321 5942

Bushwalking federations

NT: Box 1938, Darwin 5794
NSW: 176 Cumberland Street, Sydney 2000. (02) 27 4206
QLD: GPO Box 1573, Brisbane 4001
SA: Box 178, Unley 5061
Tas.: Box 190, Launceston 7250
Vic.: GPO Box 815f, Melbourne 3001
WA: 2 Pearl Parade, Scarborough 6019

Youth Hostels associations

NT: Box 39900, Winnellie 5789. (089) 84 3902
NSW: 355 Kent Street, Sydney 2000. (02) 29 5068
Qld: 462 Queen Street, Brisbane 4000. (07) 831 2022
SA: 1 Sturt Street, Adelaide 5000. (08) 51 5583
Tas.: 28 Criterion Street, Hobart 7000. (002) 34 9617
Vic.: 205 King Street, Melbourne 3000. (03) 67 7991
WA: 257 Adelaide Terrace, Perth 6000. (09) 325 5844

Acknowledgments

The publishers and editors are deeply indebted to administrators, interpretation officers and rangers of the various national parks services. Countless people spent long hours supplying or verifying information. Others assisted in planning the touring photographer's itineraries, or gave him considerable help in the field.

Thanks are also due to the staff of the National Herbarium, Royal Botanic Gardens, Sydney, for their assistance in plant identification, and to botanist A. R. Rodd.

Reference sources: The publishers acknowledge their indebtedness for information gained from the following books: *Atlas of Australian Resources* (Division of National Mapping); *Australia, a Timeless Grandeur*, Helen Grasswill (Landsdowne Press); *Australian Vegetation*, R. H. Groves, ed. (Cambridge University Press); *Australia's Endangered Species*, Derrick Ovington (Cassell); *Australia's 100 Years of National Parks* (NSW National Parks and Wildlife Service); *Complete Book of Australian Mammals*, Ronald Strahan, ed. (Angus and Robertson); *Discover Australia's National Parks*, Robert Raymond (Ure Smith); *Discover Australia's National Parks and Naturelands*, Michael and Irene Morcombe (Landsdowne Press); *Life on Earth*, David Attenborough (Reader's Digest-Collins-BBC); *National Parks of New South Wales*, Alan Fairley (Rigby); *National Parks of New South Wales* (Gregory's); *National Parks of Queensland*, Tony Groom (Cassell); *National Parks of Victoria*, Alan Fairley (Rigby); *National Parks of Victoria* (Gregory's); *National Parks of Western Australia*, C. F. H. Jenkins (National Parks Authority of WA); *Regional Landscapes of Australia*, Nancy and Andrew Learmonth (Angus and Robertson); *The Face of Australia*, C. F. Laseron, revised by J. N. Jennings (Angus and Robertson); *The Franklin Blockade*, Robin Tindale and Pam Waud, eds (Wilderness Society); *The Heritage of Australia* (Macmillan, Australian Heritage Commission); *The Value of National Parks* (Australian Conservation Foundation).

Photographs
The cover picture and most other photographs were taken by Robin Morrison, except for: (t = top, c = centre, b = bottom, l = left, r = right) 1: J. M. La Roque/Auscape. 2: Denis Daring/Auscape. 6-7: Jean-Paul Ferrero/Auscape. 11: t, Richard Woldendorp; b, Research School of Earth Sciences, ANU. 20: b, Photo Index. 28-9: Richard Woldendorp. 30: b, Dept of Conservation Forests & Lands, Vic. 31: l, cb, Sutherland Shire Library. 32: tl, bl & br, Dept of Conservation Forests & Lands, Vic. 33: tl, Ian Morris, Australian NPWS; br, Queensland NPWS. 34: Tasmanian NPWS. 35: cl, Tasmanian NPWS; tr, Bob Mossel; br, Jeffery Cutting. 36: t, Queensland NPWS; b, Dept of Conservation Forests & Lands, Vic. 37: Conservation Commission of the NT. 38: tl & bl, Hans & Judy Beste; tr, Stephen Donellan; br, R. C. Lewis, CSIRO Division of Entomology. 39: tl, R. & A. Williams, National Photographic Index; tc & tr, Hans & Judy Beste; br, Ralph & Daphne Keller. 40: r, and 41: tl & br, Dept of Conservation Forests & Lands, Vic. 41: bc, Graham Robertson; tr, New South Wales NPWS. 42: t, C. Veitch. 48-51: Bob Mossel. 70: l, Gunther Deichmann/Auscape; tr, Jean-Paul Ferrero/Auscape; cr, Hans & Judy Beste/Auscape; br, C. A. Henley/Auscape. 71: l, Jean-Paul Ferrero/Auscape; tr, C. A. Henley/Auscape; br, Graham Robertson/Auscape. 72: tl, Jack & Lindsay Cupper/Auscape; bl, L. Robinson/National Photographic Index; tr, Jean-Paul Ferrero/Auscape; br, Hans & Judy Beste/Auscape. 73: l and tc, Graeme Chapman/Auscape; tr, M. P. Kahl/Auscape; br, Lindsay Cupper/Auscape. 74-5: SA National Parks & Wildlife Service. 78-9, 81-3: Bill Bachman. 114: tl, Hans & Judy Beste/Auscape; others, Jean-Paul Ferrero/Auscape. 115: tl, Hans & Judy Beste/Auscape; others, Jean-Paul Ferrero/Auscape. 116: tl, Jean-Paul Ferrero/Auscape; bl, Hans & Judy Beste/Auscape; tr, Graeme Chapman/Auscape. 117: bc, G. Cheers/ANT; others, Hans & Judy Beste/Auscape. 118-9: Vic. Dept of Conservation Forests & Lands. 134: tl, and 135: Michael Patterson. 152: l, C. A. Henley/Auscape; tr, Robin Morrison; br, J. Burt/ANT. 153: tl, tc, Esther Beaton/Auscape; cl, Graeme Chapman/Auscape; bl, Michael Seyfort/ANT; tr, Robin Morrison; br, Otto Rogge/ANT. 154: tl, Jean-Paul Ferrero/Auscape; bl and tr, C. A. Henley/Auscape; br, Geoff Moon/Auscape. 155: tl and cr, Jean-Paul Ferrero/Auscape; bl, L. Robinson/National Photographic Index; tr, Esther Beaton/Auscape; br, R. H. Green/National Photographic Index. 156-7: Rodney Musch.

Typesetting by Smithys
433 Kent Street, Sydney 2000

Printed and bound in 1987 by Dai Nippon Ptg Co. Ltd, Hong Kong